BEYOND
What Am I And What Does It Matter?

Thane Cooper

BEYOND BEING
What Am I And What Does It Matter?

This edition published in 2015
by Tandava Press

Cover image by Thane Cooper
Cover layout by Natasha Rivers

All correspondence to the publisher at
tandavapress@gmail.com

ISBN: 9873806-8-5
ISBN-13: 978-0-9873806-8-5

Printed in Australia

Tandava Press

To my son, Aiden

Acknowledgements

To David, thank you for your complete involvement throughout the writing process.

To Nicole, thank you for your love and support.

To Stephen, thank you for your critique of the final draft.

To Lynette, thank you for proof reading the first draft.

To my family and friends, thank you for your interest, input and encouragement.

To Tandava Press, thank you for your spirit of service.

My heartfelt thanks to all. You made it possible.

You have a mind, you have a body; but are you
that mind and body?
Indeed, what is mind and what is body?
Certainly, the power of consciousness reveals both,
but what is consciousness and what is its
relationship to you?
What are you with consciousness?
What are you without it?
What are you … exactly?

Contents

Preface

Let me make a confession. For most of my life I had no inkling about self-realisation; it wasn't a thought, let alone a goal.

Had I been asked, "What are you?" no doubt I would have been content to respond, "A human being". There was no thought that I was anything other than the person I had always taken myself to be. As for any suggestion that a universe existed within me; that would have baffled me. I could have identified a few subconscious thoughts and feelings, but nothing approaching a universe.

Never in my wildest dreams could I have imagined writing a book about self-realisation, asking questions such as '*What* are you?' and claiming that you are limitless and not the person you think you are. Yet, that is the situation I find myself in.

It's only fair that I offer some sort of explanation as to how I arrived at this point.

〜

Looking back, I wasn't different to other people. As a young man I was keen on making my way in the world and enjoying the good life. I wanted to advance my professional career, develop my personal relationships, gather a wide range of experiences and accumulate as many financial assets as possible. Like many people around me, I had ambition and wanted to succeed.

Presumably, I would have stayed on this path but for an interesting set of experiences which caused me to reappraise my approach to life and the direction it was taking me.

I had accepted employment in a new city and was keen to meet the challenges involved. Initially enthusiastic, I quickly discovered that the position fell short of my expectations. My dislike for the job grew and spread to the city itself. I realised that I had made a mistake and was keen to put the experience behind me and make a fresh start somewhere else.

That was the idea, but things didn't turn out that way. Rather than make a quick getaway, I found myself cooling my heels for a seemingly interminable period. As the months dragged on, my usually robustly positive and enthusiastic approach to life faded and my desire to extricate myself turned to desperation. I recall feeling, for the first time in my life, miserably unhappy. I was so depressed that my usual pleasures couldn't give me any relief.

As my frame of mind darkened, I realised that I couldn't continue like this. Something had to give. In an effort to regain some control I began investigating how I had managed to arrive at this low point. After much soul-searching I realised that while the unhappiness had been triggered by my situation, it actually had its source in my mind and, in particular, in my attachments, beliefs and expectations. Inadvertently, I was the author of my own unhappiness.

While I wasn't necessarily unreasonable in having these expectations, they were nevertheless the cause of my unhappiness: without them I wouldn't be in the state I was in.

This insight was not only a revelation but afforded me a possible solution: if I couldn't change my situation, I could always change my expectations.

The insight was novel but also disconcerting as I didn't know if I would end up being stuck in an unacceptable situation. In the end I didn't have a choice. The unhappiness was so severe that I had to do something and so I acted on the insight. I willingly relinquished the expectations which only a short time beforehand had seemed so crucial, but were now so detrimental to my well-being.

I certainly had to swallow a lot of pride, but I didn't let it deter me. Rather than pursue my expectations, I resolved to make the most of each moment as it presented itself. I didn't give myself the luxury of pining for moments that were never to be. I stopped resisting my situation.

I wasn't sure what the result would be ... but to my relief I started to feel better. While I may not have been in great shape, I was, nonetheless, on the road to recovery. I had identified the source of my problem – my expectations – and had taken whatever responsibility I could.

~

Shortly thereafter an incredible thing happened, which I can best describe as an epiphany.

I was lying down one evening, not thinking anything in particular, when the most blissful serenity, the likes of which I had never experienced before, flooded my body and mind. I was amazed that this serenity had arisen out of a background of unhappiness.

I didn't have any explanation for this experience at the time but I was acutely aware that it was my first exposure to genuine happiness. While words cannot share the actual experience, it was a pivotal moment in my life.

Miraculously, my unhappiness dissolved and I intuitively knew that real happiness couldn't be discovered in money, possessions, pleasures or even people ... but only in the self. I knew that happiness wasn't a product of external experiences but was intrinsic to *what* I am and that there was nothing more that I wanted in life than to be happy.

Even now, all these years later, that serenity has stayed with me. It is a permanent expression of my life.

~

This experience was the catalyst for my journey of self-discovery. I didn't know what self was but I was committed to realising my reality. No obstacles would be too great to overcome.

At first, my attention was drawn to any unhappiness I experienced. While my newfound happiness never left me, I would periodically notice the odd twinge of unhappiness arising as a reaction to something I didn't like. However, rather than blame the unpleasant feeling on my situation or other people, or try to escape it, I embraced it as an opportunity to learn.

Regardless of how much I might have disliked the sensation, I would make it a priority to explore the unhappiness. Interestingly, I discovered that while the particular situation had revealed the unhappiness, invariably its source could be traced to an underlying and usually subconscious expectation I held of achieving a desire or avoiding a fear ... my unspoken assumption about how life should be.

By becoming acutely aware of the assumption and the unhappiness it caused, I would naturally stop clinging to the expectation. I quickly discovered that the unhappiness would disappear too. I further discovered that if the expectation was completely relinquished, the particular unhappiness it generated would also dissolve ... never to be experienced again ... ever.

In the process of learning the lessons of unhappiness my experience of life was greatly transformed, but perhaps even more significantly, through these lessons I was unwittingly drawn towards the realisation of self.

~

In tandem with my appreciation of the opportunity that unhappiness afforded, I was also acutely aware of the profound sense of happiness I experienced, even when, paradoxically, I felt unhappy. Acute awareness of unhappiness and happiness were crucial to my journey of self-discovery.

As my mind was increasingly freed from the machinations of unhappiness, the more the glow of the underlying happiness flooded my life. I found that instead of getting caught up in the usual busyness which occupied my mind, I naturally gravitated towards the silence of that underlying happiness. Rather than give attention to the thoughts, I was aware of the profound silence beneath them.

As this beautiful silence engulfed my mind, I became aware of a subtle energy in my body, which, owing to my focus on daily preoccupations and more conspicuous sensations, had previously been overlooked.

My experience of this energy increased until it became an abiding presence in my life. The energy was not only present as I went about my daily activities, but in meditation would become intense and be accompanied by white light (either flashes or a glow) and profound insights.

The existence of this energy was so striking that I instinctively knew that it was highly significant to my journey. However, despite the bliss of abiding in this energy, I couldn't penetrate it to understand what it was or what it signified.

While the energy revealed that my spiritual quest was the realisation of self, I began to sense that my search was stalling and that I was in need of direction.

～

There was no one around me who could offer advice and so in deep meditation I would seek guidance. Invariably, the answer that would emerge out of the silence was "travel".

Fortunately, it became possible to heed the advice and I travelled the world. I learnt many lessons en route, but even on the eve of returning home still hadn't found the guidance that I was looking for.

On the flight home from India to Australia I started to read a book I had purchased on a whim the day before. It was called *I Am That* and contained the teachings of Sri Maharaj Nisargadatta. I was immediately struck by the profundity of the text, the like of which I hadn't experienced before.

I instinctively knew that Nisargadatta would give me the guidance I had been looking for.

While the book was challenging to understand, I gained many insights, none more pertinent to my search than how to approach the energy I had encountered. I realised that rather than cling to the energy as I had been doing, I needed to observe it as though from a distance.

I wholeheartedly put this advice into practice. Amazingly, in so doing, I began to perceive the energy in its correct perspective and understand its significance. Just through observing I started to see everything in a different light. By simply observing I became aware of what lay beyond the energy ... and beyond being.

During the many months of intensive meditative practice my progress was gradual but steady; however, when the moment of realisation finally dawned it was sudden and instantaneous. The shell in which I had been encased was cracked. Everything was absorbed by the observing; inner and outer were dissolved. I was all. I was nothing. I was beyond all and nothing.

In absolute silence, self was realised. It was the most amazing moment of my life.

~

The resulting transformation was astounding. I was complete and lacked nothing. My mind was clear. My perspective was transformed.

Since then, my life is completely different. It is a simple life and it is a wonderful life. It is the life I love.

Happiness, the like of which can't be imagined, is reality of every moment of my life. Not only is there a lightness of being but there is an ease to life. Things fall into place as they should and must.

As I write these words I can honestly say that unhappiness is a vague memory.

⁓

Having arrived at this peculiarly beautiful but entirely natural vantage, there is nothing more that I want to do than share this bounty with others. This book is the result. It is my attempt to share some insights that come from self-realisation and the means by which you may experience self-realisation for yourself.

Crucially, this book isn't based on what I have read or been taught, nor is it indebted to any particular spiritual philosophy, religious tradition or scientific school of thought. It is based on my direct experience.

I have tried to write the text in a user-friendly manner; however, given the depth of the subject matter, it can't be grasped in a cursory reading. Profound issues are raised which will require considered reflection ... and more.

The book won't necessarily say what you want or hope to hear, but rather what you need to hear ... at least once in your life.

⁓

Despite any failings in the text, this book is an expression of my love.

I want you to know that you don't have to be unhappy. More than that, I want you to be supremely happy. I don't want you to live an unfulfilling life. I want you to live the life you love.

I can't give you the solution to the problems you may have, but I can tell you that you already have the answers. The journey that you need to take is within. Ask yourself one simple but startling question – *"What am I?"*

In the course of exploring your reality, all will be resolved. Once self is realised, the clarity of pure and unobstructed love will shine brightly and light your world.

There is no higher good that you can desire.

⌣

I invite you to come on the most rewarding journey of your life.

Introduction

This book is about you. It is an exploration of your reality. It is the most important journey that you can take.

Many people, though, will not see it that way. Caught up in the practicalities of life – going to work, raising children, paying the bills – and being time short, they will see it as a theoretical pursuit of little relevance, significance or importance. However, nothing could be further from the truth.

Self-realisation is the most transformative event you can experience. It not only profoundly changes the way you perceive life but deeply affects the type of life you lead.

Whatever your situation, there is nothing better you can do for yourself and those around you than realise your reality.

~

Of course, it isn't necessary to explore your reality ... most people don't. Like them, you can continue as you have been. However, there is a price to pay.

While you remain ignorant of your reality you will continue to be ruled by circumstances beyond your control and suffer the stresses presented by those circumstances.

The price of this self-ignorance is unhappiness. It is no exaggeration to say that all your unhappiness can be traced to the fact that you don't know what you are.

⌐

It is true that you can seek, through pleasurable activities or general busyness, distraction from unhappiness. However, a nagging sense that something is missing in your life will follow you. It may be expressed as an undefinable longing – whether boredom, loneliness or melancholy – or the feeling that you aren't making the most of your life or don't know what to do with your life. It may also be expressed as deep sadness or profound unhappiness. However described, it points to the fact that you don't feel full and complete.

Even though you may not always be conscious of this discontent, it casts a long and deep shadow across your life. In fact, your life has unwittingly been lived in its shadow.

That discontent may drive you, on one hand, to become wealthy, achieve great things or be the envy of others, or on the other hand, to become addicted to drugs, food or gambling … but regardless of your means of escape, that underlying sense of neediness continues to pursue you.

⌐

Actually, the sense of completeness that you most want in life can't be realised through the usual run of activities. Why? Because what is missing is not more possessions, more experiences, more busyness, more achievements, more love, more anything ... but rather the realisation of what you are.

You are the missing piece of the jigsaw which is your life. If you don't realise what you are, the picture will never – can never – be complete.

If you are to be free of all discontent and realise the true bounty that life has to offer, you must know what you are.

There is no other way. Nothing but self-realisation can fill and satisfy you, and give you that sense of wholeness and completeness you most desire. What is caused by self-ignorance can only be remedied by self-realisation. There is no substitute.

If you are to find complete peace, love, happiness and freedom in this life, then you must realise your reality. '*What* am I?' is the one question you must ask and answer.

～

Undoubtedly, self-realisation is the most significant event you can experience in life. Nothing will be the same again.

Once you realise exactly what you are, you are filled with a profound sense of wholeness, unlike anything you have previously experienced. You lack nothing, you need nothing, you want nothing. You are all you have ever needed or ever could have wanted. You are all and sufficient.

Your mind is filled with an intuitive clarity and all appears clear and simple. You are in complete harmony with all that happens. Problems cease, stress vanishes and life presents no difficulties. Life is joy.

Remnants of your unrewarding life drop away and your world opens up to you in ways you could never have imagined possible. You live your passion and do what you love. You realise your potential.

～

Without doubt, the best thing that you can do for yourself and those around you is to realise your reality. The best thing that those around you can do for themselves is realise theirs.

Self-realisation is the light which transforms. It is the ultimate good.

～

Rest assured that self-realisation is eminently possible. Make no mistake; your reality is available to you now.

As you are the destination and the goal, you don't have to do anything, learn anything or become anything. You just have to realise what you already are.

I'm not saying that you won't have challenges to overcome. You will. However, those challenges don't arise because of what you have to gain but what you have to let go.

It is only your mistaken assumptions about self and world which obscure your reality. Stop assuming that your world is what it isn't and that you are what you cannot be and your reality will be clear.

The task is not insurmountable. With desire it is inevitable.

~

This book will lead you on a step by step journey to the very depths of being ... and beyond.

By peeling back the layers of mistaken assumption it lays bare the indisputable fact of your reality. No leaps of faith are taken because none are required. Through a common-sense, practical approach it reveals that you are much more than you have ever assumed yourself to be.

The genres of philosophy, psychology, science, spirituality and self-enrichment will be traversed, but the journey is not beholden to any ideology or tradition. Instead, you will be guided on a stimulating journey of self-discovery, which requires no prior spiritual or scientific understanding.

While the coverage of subject matter is both in-depth and all-encompassing, the treatment is well-articulated and carefully explained. As such, the book represents a solid introduction if you have never pondered your reality before but, equally, represents an indispensable guide if you are an advanced seeker on your journey of self-discovery.

Although there is no quick fix, *Beyond Being* offers the shortest, clearest and most practical route to self-realisation available.

—

Regardless of your background, if you are ready to stop living in the shadow of unhappiness, have the courage to discard even the most ingrained but ultimately false ideas, and have the desire to explore what you've never explored before, then I invite you to realise what you are.

If living life at its fullest and most meaningful, being serenely free and one with all is in anyway a worthwhile goal … then realise your reality.

The real journey is within.

The Challenge

To read this book, a genuine interest in questioning your own long-held assumptions and openness to fresh perspectives is crucial. Without this inquisitiveness, this book isn't for you.

If you don't have this natural curiosity you will be content with your current understanding and will see no benefit in delving any further to realise what you are.

On the other hand, if you have an open mind and a desire to learn, this book will be a revelation, hopefully changing your life as much as it has changed mine. While the ideas will be challenging, with due consideration they will resonate within you and strike a resounding chord. What might initially seem perplexing will become obvious.

As layers of mistaken assumption are peeled away, increasingly profound insights into the nature of world and self will be revealed and you will find that you are naturally drawn to a new way of being.

The only ingredient you need to bring is an open mind which desires to understand afresh. With this desire, *Beyond Being* will take you on a profound journey into the deepest reaches of being and beyond. And with this desire you will come to the realisation of what you are … timeless, spaceless, limitless, and altogether beyond being.

While it may seem like a fanciful claim at this juncture, once self is realised your life will be filled with a deep and permanent joy. Unhappiness will be forgotten. Nothing will be the same again.

The success of this journey depends on you. With desire the journey is effortless. Without desire it is impossible.

~

This book is a journey to the self, to the essence of what you are.

While 'who' you are is constantly changing – a child who studies, an adult who works or a senior who is retired – 'what' you are is that essence which bridges all the changing versions of 'who' you are and, indeed, makes them possible. *What* you are is your indisputable reality.

This journey to *what* you are is unlike any other, because you already are the destination. As such, there is no distance to be traversed, you just need to realise what you are … already.

The journey doesn't attempt the impossible of reaching what you are, but instead focuses on identifying the mistaken assumptions which prevent you from realising your reality. In the absence of those assumptions your reality is clear and obvious. You arrive at the startling realisation of what you are.

The journey cannot affect your reality (that is unshakeable) but it will dramatically affect the ideas which obscure the clear perception of self.

~

While many assumptions obscure your reality, they can be broadly categorised as assumptions relating to world and assumptions relating to self.

The first assumption to be considered in this book is the belief that the world is a physical reality. It will be suggested that the appearance of tangibility exists as a mental image in mind and is actually an illusion. It will be argued that whatever is experienced, discovered or understood is a mental appearance, and that nothing is a physical reality.

This perspective not only requires a reappraisal of assumptions regarding the nature of physical matter but, perhaps more significantly, an appreciation of the vast depths of mind.

The second assumption that will be considered is the belief that what you are can be discovered as an object. To the contrary, it will be claimed that you aren't an object you perceive, but rather that which perceives the object. You aren't a body you can observe, a set of behaviours you can analyse, a sequence of ideas you can think, or a stream of sensations you can feel. They point to your reality but you are none of those pointers.

This perspective is crucial if you are to realise that your reality is beyond mind and matter, body and soul, or any other mental image you may form.

~

The latter part of the book is more practical in nature. It provides guidance as to how your unfathomable reality can be realised.

It identifies some of the profound insights that can be gained from perceiving unhappiness as friend rather than foe. It shares some meditation techniques and how they can be practiced in daily life, all with a view to expanding the scope of your conscious awareness. And through a process of identifying all that you cannot be – from body to thoughts, memories to the underlying sense of existence – it explores the deepest layers of being, drawing you closer to the reality of self.

~

Once free of false assumptions you realise that what you are is not just another perceivable object in a world of perceivable objects, but instead more like an eye that can see everything except itself.

That unimaginable reality can't be perceived, imagined or conceptualised. No ideas – whether spirit, soul or energy – capture that reality. You are what you are with those mental images but, more significantly, you are what you are without them.

Yet it is your reality and it can be realised.

⌣

That said, more than mere verbal formulations, self-realisation demands direct experience. No one can teach you what you are. You must realise what you are for yourself. There is no other way.

It's up to you to question even your most fundamental, but ultimately mistaken, assumptions. It's up to you to harness the potential of your conscious awareness. It's up to you to move beyond the words to the experience.

This book will guide you but the journey has to be your own. Real progress isn't determined by what you read but by what you realise for yourself.

⌣

Undoubtedly, desire is the crucial ingredient. Only with sincere desire will you cross the gulf which separates you from what you most seek ... you. The result: intuitive clarity, wholeness and complete harmony.

If you have the desire, then I invite you to embark on the most fascinating journey of your life.

The challenge is yours.

1 Question your assumptions

Many years ago there was a village where the people revered the sun. Its movements had dominated their lives for generations. They praised its rising in the morning, solemnly observed its setting in the evening and pondered its disappearance at night.

One day a traveller came to the village. He spoke of foreign lands, marvellous sights, and knew of many things. News of his arrival quickly reached the village priest, who promptly extended an invitation for the visitor to attend the sunset ceremony.

As dusk drew near, the villagers gathered to honour their sun and implore it not to desert them, but despite their pleas, darkness soon fell.

The priest exclaimed to the traveller, "You see, our beloved sun has left our skies; we pray it will bless us again with its light." Looking pensively, he added, "They say you are a wise man, so can you tell us why our sun won't stay in the sky?"

The man looked at the priest and quietly replied, "Do not be concerned for your prayers have already been answered. Your sun has not moved; it's still shining high."

Surprised, the priest said, "Friend, but do you not see that our sun has departed. Already it is dark and nightfall is upon us."

The man plainly responded, "The fact that it's dark isn't an act of the sun. It's you who have moved and caused darkness to appear."

Thinking that these words were nonsense, the priest demanded, "Why speak these untruths? I haven't moved. We both saw our dear sun sink below that horizon. It is our sun which has left us and darkened our skies."

The visitor nodded his head and said, "While all seems to be in darkness your sun is still shining. Your sun hasn't moved; it's still up in the sky. The appearance of movement is just a trick of perception. Question your assumptions and all will be clear."

The priest threw his arms in the air and looked around at the crowd, bellowing, "Enough of his riddles. Take him out of my sight. I've tired of his nonsense … we all know that it's night."

The villagers agreed with the priest; what he said was clearly correct. The sun had indeed moved and left them in darkness. It obviously wasn't a trick of perception.

There was no doubt that this traveller wasn't as wise as they had taken him to be or else he was trying to make fools of them by his mischievous lies.

As they led the man out of the village he turned and said, "Friends, the sun doesn't move – that's only an illusion. It's the spin of the earth which causes confusion. Just consider the fact ..." But no one was listening: they knew that this man was a fool and their priest was right.

The man left the village and was quickly forgotten. The villagers continued their customs as though nothing had happened. They attended their ceremonies and prayed to their sun.

That is, all but one, who remembered that man and the odd words he spoke, and silently wondered, "Maybe my beliefs have been wrong and that curious old man was right".

In time that doubt grew and opened her mind. And she came to see sunsets in an entirely new light.

~

It's not surprising that the villagers could look at a sunset and believe that the sun moved across the sky and out of sight. It certainly appeared that way to them. And it's equally understandable that they would resist any suggestion that the sun didn't move. Their common sense would tell them that this can't be right.

However, despite the people's strong conviction, we know otherwise ... the sun neither rises nor sets. We know that the seeming motion of the sun is an illusion caused by the rotation of the earth.

While we can understand how the villagers could believe that the sun moved across the sky, we know that it is a mistaken belief: reasonable yes, but it is still a misunderstanding.

~

While you yourself may not harbour the belief that the sun moves across the sky, there are undoubtedly many other assumptions that you nurture about yourself and your world which are not correct.

This isn't surprising. While your assumptions may seem self-evident, with more information and insight they could be revealed as misunderstandings.

After all, the possibility of mistake is inherent in any assumption. And when that assumption results from inadvertence, the risk of mistake is greatly increased.

~

Certainly, if history is any guide, it has been remarkably common for assumptions which have been championed as understanding to subsequently be revealed as misunderstanding. Assumptions that the earth was flat or the centre of the universe readily come to mind.

We can be sure that even now some of the most fundamental assumptions of our own time are also mistaken.

Arguably, the more fundamental (and presumably the more inadvertent and untested) the assumption, the more likely it is a misunderstanding.

~

That said, I wouldn't want you to form the impression that misunderstandings are in any way negative though. To the contrary, they are necessary steps in the learning process.

Once misunderstanding is recognised for what it is, deeper understanding is born. Misunderstanding is problematic only when stubbornly championed as true understanding.

This inflexible type of thinking impairs the learning process and becomes an obstacle to further understanding.

Misunderstanding isn't the problem, inflexible thinking is.

~

Throughout the course of this book I will touch on several issues which may challenge deeply ingrained beliefs you have about self and world.

These ideas may be disconcerting and you may end up rejecting them. However, by at least considering them you may come to recognise long held misunderstandings that you have inadvertently maintained.

The benefit of that recognition cannot be overestimated. Just as darkness dissolves in the presence of light, once you recognise misunderstanding, it ceases. Then fresh and exciting levels of understanding are revealed.

When all misunderstanding is recognised, only the clarity of understanding remains. Then you see things as they are, for what they are.

My challenge to you is not to nurture misunderstanding but to be free of it.

⌢

Your beliefs about self and world may seem reasonable, but when challenged what is your response?

Are you like the majority of those villagers who are dismissive of new insights and cling to their customary beliefs? Are you mildly interested but ultimately not prepared to change your long held assumptions? Or are you willing to recognise misunderstanding and open up to new dimensions of understanding?

Are you that one person who comes to see all in an entirely new light?

2 The world as a concept

So, what might be a mistaken assumption you inadvertently believe?

I guess if you are like most people, you probably think of 'the world' as the universe and solar system. More specifically you might think of planet earth with its various continents, geographical formations, climatic conditions and abundance of life forms.

You have many opinions about the state of this world and there are undoubtedly many things you would like to preserve or change. However, underpinning all these impressions is the idea of a common world, which is observed, experienced and shared by all.

⁓

The idea of a world common to all, a world consisting of one planet, moon and sun is so entrenched in our current understanding that we cannot conceive of anything but the existence of this one common world.

It seems to be so self-evident that we don't even think to ask if this assumption is correct. However, that is precisely the assumption I want to consider with you.

Is there a world common to all?

Your instinct is most likely to say, "Yes, of course", but if so let me ask you a supplementary question. Where is this common world?

You may think that this question is a little unusual, but to draw your attention to the seriousness of the query, I will repeat it. Where is this common world you assume exists?

Think about your answer.

~

Your response will probably be, "Well, here it is around us. It's this common world we observe and share".

Obviously, this would be an intelligent response and reflects generally accepted wisdom. You might even be so convinced by this response that you wonder how there could be any doubt that 'the world' is all around us. However, with just a little examination the inadequacy of this response should become apparent.

~

Consider this ...

Isn't it true that whatever common world you may think you are pointing out is actually only ever *your* world? It is a world that *you* experience with *your* senses and which only *you* know. It is *your* private experience.

Even if you think you are pointing out a common world to me, it is not so. Whatever world I observe you pointing out is only ever a part of *my* world.

I only know the world *I* sense and experience ... *my* world. I do not know *the* world you are trying to point out.

⁓

The only world you can know is your world. You cannot know mine. No matter how much you search for my world you can only realise yours. Whatever you discover only exists in your world. Whatever you do only expands the frontiers of your world. You cannot cross the boundary that separates your world from mine.

Similarly, I cannot know your world. I can't enter your world and experience what you think or feel. I can never know how a rose smells to you, how food tastes to you, how the sun's rays feel on your skin. I will never experience your joy or pain.

Only you know what it is like to live your life, sense your senses, feel your feelings, think your thoughts, and experience ... your world. Your world is your unique perspective, your private affair. My world is my subjective and personal experience.

⁓

You can certainly attempt to describe the world you experience to me, but no matter how detailed and expressive those words may be, they cannot impart the actual experience of your world.

Based on the words you use, I might be able to form an idea about your world, but that idea is just another aspect of my world; it is not the experience of yours.

Only you know what your world is like for you. I don't.

~

In fact, our worlds are so private that we cannot even share our experiences. We can observe a sunset and say we shared the experience, but actually your experience of the sunset is unique to you and different to mine.

Even if we were to embrace, we don't share the same experience. You know how it feels to embrace me, but I know nothing about your experience. I only know how it feels to embrace you.

You might give me some of the food you are eating and while I can taste it, I don't know how it tastes to you.

Owing to the similarity of our physical makeup, our experiences may be similar, yet they are not the same. Inherent differences in timing, location and context mean that no two experiences can ever be exactly the same.

We may even use the same words to describe what we see, taste, hear, smell and feel, but the actual experience is still different … same in description, but different in experience.

~

In fact, our respective worlds are made up of subjective experiences which are not common to all. None of what you experience is exactly replicated in my world or any other. Your world is your unique experience. My world is my unique experience.

However, the fact that people may use the same words to describe what are actually different experiences creates the illusion that we live in a world which is common to all – 'the world'.

In point of fact though, rather than live in the one common world, we all experience and, indeed, live in our own personal and private worlds.

~

Actually, your world is so subjectively yours that if you ceased to exist, your world would cease to exist with you. And more intriguingly, if hypothetically you never existed then your world would never have existed either.

Just think about that for a moment; if you never existed, nothing in your world would have existed either … nothing!

And everything which you may currently view as 'the common world' would not have come into existence.

Why? Because the world you experience isn't common to all; it is your subjective experience. It is unique to you.

~

The implications of this line of thought are far reaching.

If you can only know your world and I can only know mine, then neither of us can know 'the world'. Like everyone else we can only experience our respective subjective worlds. No one can experience a common objective world – the world.

Now the point is this: surely a common objective world which can't be experienced by anyone must only exist as pure conjecture; it exists as an idea which can never be proved.

And if this objective world can never be experienced, let alone proved, can it reasonably be said to exist? As such, isn't it a product of pure imagination … a myth?

You can draw your own conclusions, however I would like to suggest that there is a strong case that 'the world' is not so much a tangible reality but a common belief. It is a concept built on an illusion of sameness, where in actuality nothing is the same.

Your world is the fact but 'the world' is your assumption.

~

At the start of this chapter, you might have thought that your belief in the existence of a common world was unshakeable, but with just some gentle probing it turns out that this assumption may be an over-simplification of the actual situation ... perhaps a misunderstanding.

Just because you observe what appears to be one earth and sun doesn't mean that there is just one common world. The situation is more complex than that. In actuality, you are observing your own world which is your personal, private and unique experience.

⁓

As everything in your world is your subjective experience, nothing in your world can be said to be common to all. I'd suggest that the assumption that you share a common world is based on an illusion ... just like the assumption of a moving sun.

3 There is a world for every mind

I am well aware that a few lines in the previous chapter claiming that there's no such thing as a common world isn't going to dispel any long standing beliefs you have that 'the world' as a physical entity does in fact exist.

After all, even as you read these words and look around you it must seem self-evident that there is a common world which we all share ... a world of physical matter which isn't just your personal experience ... a real objective world which is the basis for any and all subjective worlds.

For this reason, the following chapters will work on dispelling the idea that 'the world' exists as a physical entity independent to what you perceive.

I am in no doubt as to the challenge that lies ahead of me but with some of your time and attention I hope, if nothing else, to share with you some interesting insights about the world you live in. You may even come to appreciate and understand the world and your place in it in different and exciting ways. And if you can personally experience the perspective that will be shared, you will be taking an important stride towards realising the supreme happiness of self-realisation.

~

I'd like to take the next step on our journey of self-discovery by continuing to explore the notion raised in the last chapter, that of *your* world.

I asked you a question *"where is the world?"* and suggested that you can't answer as the only world you can identify is your world. I noted that this world of yours is the only world you experience and that you can't share the experience of your world with anyone else. Your world at all times remains a personal and private experience, unique to you.

That being the case, I would now like to ask you another question ... where is *your* world?

~

At this point I guess you might be thinking that you can quite confidently gesticulate and say, "Well, here it is all around me. It's this world I observe and know."

That would certainly seem a logical proposition. After all if you only know and observe your world, then it must be this world around you ... surely.

This assumption seems to be persuasive but let's test the theory.

If we are both in a room and are asked the location of our respective worlds, based on the above logic you will claim that your world is all around you, while I will also make the same claim.

This presents a dilemma. If your world is different from my world, how can both our worlds be around us in that room? If our worlds are physical realities, how is it that they can occupy the same space?

Is your world all around you or is my world all around me? Or is there another possibility that we have overlooked?

Could it be that our respective worlds are not actually located where we think they are?

⁓

As you might have guessed, I'd like to suggest that there is another approach. Let me share my perspective with you.

If I was asked 'where is my world?' I would not answer "all around me". Instead I would confidently respond "in my mind".

If questioned, I would add that my world appears to be all around me, yet in actuality the entirety of my world exists as a perception playing out on the screen of my mind ... in fact, it is the screen of my mind. It seems to be a physical reality but in actuality it is a mental phenomenon.

As such, while it would seem as though our respective worlds were around us in that room, apparently occupying the same space, in fact your world exists in your mind and my world exists in mine. Our worlds may be projected onto the seemingly same space but they don't exist in space, they actually exist in mind.

While our worlds may appear to be physical phenomena, existing in 'physical' time and space, I want to suggest that they are actually more like mental phenomena, existing in mind ... where time and space are also interesting aspects of mind.

—

This is a challenging way of perceiving your world ... and everyone else's ... however, it is a proposition that I would like you to ponder very carefully.

Your world doesn't actually exist all around you; it only exists in your mind. It is your unique perspective.

—

This proposition not only challenges your assumptions about the nature of your world but perhaps even more significantly, the nature of your mind.

It may be tempting to think of your mind as this relatively insignificant phenomenon existing inside your head, observing and reacting to the world around it. However, to appreciate the perspective that I am trying to share, this assumption needs to be thoroughly questioned.

I would suggest that your mind is not bounded by the physical apparatus of your head. It has no such boundary. And rather than being insignificant, I want to suggest that your mind is, in fact, vast ... so vast that the world you observe is actually cradled within the immensity of your mind.

I want to further suggest that your mind is so profound that its deep depths extend beyond the appearance of your world. Those depths were present during the very first appearance of matter. In fact, your mind is so deep that *all* matter is actually an appearance in mind.

Those deep depths of your mind are the same deep depths of all other minds, and so everything that has ever existed is an expression of the depths of the one mind.

~

Yes, this is another challenging perspective which will be developed through the course of the book. At this stage though, I just want to alert you to the fact that I will be challenging your assumptions about the nature of mind.

Your mind is not insignificant. It is vast and all encompassing.

~

It follows that if your world exists in the vastness of your mind and your mind is all encompassing ... then nothing that you have ever observed (can ever observe), have ever known (can ever know), have ever experienced (can ever experience), have ever sensed (can ever sense) exists beyond your mind. All exists within the ambit of mind.

As such, physical objects and external events you perceive are not separate to your mind, but rather intrinsic to it ... so intrinsic that they do not exist without your mind.

Those seemingly physical and external realities are neither physical nor external. They are actually mental images which appear in your mind. They are more properly described as mental appearances. Sure, they may appear physical and external, but if you scratch beneath that appearance, that isn't their underlying nature.

⁓

Yes, a challenging issue which we will consider at length during the course of the book. All I ask is that you are prepared to question your assumptions.

Physical matter and external events are not as they appear. Like your world, they are mental phenomena appearing in mind.

⁓

I appreciate that these concepts may be difficult to grasp, however, we will work through them carefully and in some detail. In so doing, I will not only expand on the concepts but through examples and exercises encourage you to experience this perspective of your world for yourself.

4 The mental image perspective

Ideally, I'd like to follow up the last chapter with our first practical exercise. However, without wanting to over-complicate matters, there is benefit if we use this chapter to articulate the theory in greater detail.

As you'll recall, so far on our journey I have called into question the existence of a world which is common to all – the world – and have asserted that anyone can only know their respective worlds. I have claimed that this personal world exists in the mind which perceives it and that its substance isn't physical.

In this chapter we'll consider how a world which is understood as mental in nature is perceived differently to a world which is physical.

~

If you assume that the universe is a physical phenomenon you will believe that it pre-existed your birth. You will believe that it is ancient and vast. You may believe that its genesis occurred through a cataclysmic event called the 'big bang'; that subsequent evolutionary processes resulted in the formation of stars and planets; and that on one known planet, Earth, these processes spurred the emergence of life in all its diversity.

You may believe that human beings emerged out of this evolutionary mix and that after countless generations you yourself were born into this world.

You will have observed your physical body grow and develop, and may closely identify with that body.

And during the course of your life you will have observed many objects and learned to call them names (star, mountain, tree, dog). You will think of them as physical realities, existing independently to you. You will believe that these independently existing objects comprise a world which is common to all.

You recognise that your body is but an insignificant dot appearing briefly in the vastness of the universe.

You know that this world will continue to exist after your death.

~

I can relate to this 'physical world' point of view. I understand how people could think like this and in many ways I don't have a problem with this perspective. However, I can't be completely content with this view as it represents a great oversimplification of the actual situation. Indeed, by just focusing on the physical it overlooks the role of mind.

Certainly every experience we have of matter is dependent on mind and, in particular, the function of perception. Mind-perception is intrinsic to the matter you sense and the physical world you are familiar with. It not only determines how matter appears to you, but if it appears to you at all. Indeed, without perception matter is not only unperceived, it is unperceivable.

Undoubtedly perception plays such a vital role in your experience of matter that mind must be a crucial factor in any accurate understanding you can formulate about the nature of the so-called physical world.

~

Perception is not only crucial to the matter you experience, but is equally crucial to the existence of matter at chemical, atomic and sub-atomic levels.

This might seem an odd claim, so please let me explain.

I'm aware that we don't usually think of perception operating at these seemingly purely physical levels, however, take the example of two hydrogen atoms. While conventional wisdom tells us that any bonding which may occur is an entirely physical process, perception is actually playing a role. How so? Well there is a rudimentary type of perceiving occurring for those hydrogen atoms to 'recognise' and interact with each other. I'm not saying that it's a conscious process, but I am saying that it's a natural and spontaneous expression of a primordial ability to perceive.

Certainly, without this basic perceptive ability such interactions would not be possible.

Interestingly, the absence of perception would not only prevent any possible bonding between the two hydrogen atoms, but would also prevent the subatomic interactions necessary to produce those atoms in the first place.

Indeed, without perception the building blocks of matter could not form, let alone develop or evolve, or ultimately be expressed as a range of appearances comprising the seemingly material world you are familiar with.

I would suggest that perceiving – albeit rudimentary, primordial and non-conscious – is crucial to all expressions of matter.

Certainly, the fact that perceiving is evident at ostensibly purely physical levels not only raises questions about the nature of matter but also about the nature of mind, and the indisputably intrinsic relationship between them.

~

Given the fundamental role of perception, I suggest that if you understand your world only from a physical perspective then you are possibly overlooking central aspects of your world. And for this reason I would like to offer some balance by introducing you to an alternative to the 'physical world' perspective.

In attempting to share this alternative perspective, we are met with some challenges up front. We are so accustomed to thinking about our worlds in terms of physical matter that, at least initially, it is difficult to come to terms with a world that isn't comprised of essentially physical material ... where the objects around us, while appearing physical, aren't actually tangible ... where all exists in mind.

However, while it is challenging it certainly is not impossible.

For me the starting point is to think of my world in terms of mental images, not solid things. So if, for example, I experience a rock, a wave breaking on the shore or a plane flying in the sky, I don't think of it as a physical reality but rather as an image which appears in my mind.

By applying this principle to everything I observe my world is thereby reduced to a collection of mental images. These images may be extremely diverse in appearance, yet they can all be comprehended as mental images.

Having developed this perspective, when I turn my attention to the alleged birth of the physical world – the 'big bang', the rapid expansion of hydrogen and helium gases, and the formation of stars – it becomes apparent that this history can also be perceived as a conceptual interpretation.

Even if, for the sake of argument, I accept that this history is, broadly speaking, accurate, I recognise that it exists as a series of mental images in my mind.

And when I enquire into the nature of these mental images it becomes apparent that they come into existence as a result of intelligence. More significantly though, they are products of consciousness.

Indeed, consciousness must be present before any of these mental images can arise.

—

As such, while it might appear that I have accurately traced the history of my physical world to its apparent birth, what I have actually done is form a series of mental images in my mind … all of which are expressions of and dependent on consciousness.

Consciousness not only gives birth to the physical world I experience … but also to my notion of the 'big bang'.

I'd suggest that if I am to understand the world I perceive then my starting point must be consciousness … and not an idea which results from that consciousness.

I encourage you to give careful consideration to this intriguing way of perceiving.

—

Without wanting to go into unnecessary detail, this alternative perspective raises some further questions. To start with … 'what is consciousness?'

Obviously, this is a deeply challenging question which I can't hope to do justice to in these few introductory remarks. However, allow me to make a couple of points.

- Consciousness is a sensation. It can be described as the sense of existence, the sense of being, the sense 'I am'. However, while we might be able to describe consciousness, it can't be comprehended as a description any more than the taste of a banana can be appreciated through a dictionary definition. Like the taste of the banana, consciousness is a sensation which must be experienced to be understood.

- As a sensation, consciousness is a mental image. Yet, as the first mental image, its appearance marks the birth of the conscious mind and its associated world of sensations and mental images. Only when consciousness arises can other sensations and mental images occur.

~

During the course of this book, we will consider the nature of consciousness in depth. However, having noted that consciousness represents the birth of the physical world I experience, we may certainly ask, 'what precedes consciousness?'

This is another highly significant question which can't be adequately addressed in a few lines. However, let me make the comment that whatever response we might give is a product of consciousness and not what actually preceded the appearance of consciousness. Indeed, what precedes consciousness is devoid of all conscious interpretation.

This isn't to say that such conceptual investigation is without benefit, but it is important to appreciate its limitations.

Whatever conceptual interpretation you arrive at isn't the reality of what existed prior to consciousness. Instead, it is an intellectual framework attempting to understand that reality. Even if the ideas are verifiable experimentally, they still don't capture the 'substance' or 'truth' of what precedes consciousness.

If you want an accurate understanding, the thinking mind with its collection of concepts – whether borrowed from science, philosophy, religion or spirituality – is not an appropriate instrument.

As such, even though I might use words such as 'depths of mind', 'non-conscious functioning', 'awareness' or 'Reality' to describe what precedes consciousness, to be properly understood this non-conscious state must be 'experienced' directly.

You will be introduced to techniques to explore these mysterious depths later in the book.

~

The emergence of consciousness out of this mysterious prior state represents the necessary conditions which give rise to the conscious mind. From that point a host of sensations start to be experienced.

At first these sensations are meaningless, but soon take shape as a marvellous array of mental images which are interpreted as a world of material objects and actual events spread across time and space.

That is the appearance, yet they all play out on the incredibly complex 'screen' which is the conscious mind.

They appear to be common to everyone, but are unique to the experiencer. They appear to be real, but are products of the senses. They appear to exist independently of consciousness, but actually arise courtesy of it.

~

While consciousness is supported, sensations are experienced and mental images are formed. The resulting world develops in depth, scope, meaning and purpose, yet only ever amounts to a collection of mental images.

However, when the sensation of consciousness ceases – as when the person dies – that world of mental images ceases with it. That seemingly physical world doesn't persist beyond the appearance of consciousness on which it depended.

Without the support of consciousness, only that mysterious state prior to consciousness remains.

Of course, consciousness doesn't end there; it continues to be experienced by other people who are still alive. Sensations continue to be experienced and worlds of mental images continue appearing.

However, at no stage is there a purely physical world common to all.

~

If this line of thought is new to you, I guess that these concepts will present some food for thought which, no doubt, will require careful consideration. That said, before we finish this chapter let's turn our attention to the most significant issue of all to ponder.

If consciousness is the support of all conscious worlds and everything that appears in that world exists as a mental image ... *what* are you?

We can't hope to answer this question in the next few lines – not the least because what you are can't be captured by any verbal formulation – however, allow me to make the following observations.

If you are nothing but a mental image, then you are a product of consciousness and you depend on that consciousness for your continued existence. Once consciousness ceases so do you.

While that is a sobering thought, it's not true to say that you are just a mental image.

Your self-image, memories, ideas, beliefs, personality and life experiences are undoubtedly mental images which are dependent on consciousness and do go into oblivion during deep sleep, unconsciousness or 'death' ... however, there is a deeper aspect to your reality which exists when you aren't conscious.

That deeper reality is non-conscious awareness. It is unaffected by the appearance and disappearance of consciousness. Yet in the right conditions it is expressed as the sensation of consciousness and the appearance of your world ... of which your body and self-image are an intrinsic part.

~

This rather complicated explanation effectively means that your world exists as a mental image appearing in consciousness ... and consciousness exists as a sensation emerging from the deeper reality of what you are.

The implication is that you are not a speck which appears in the world, but 'the' world is a speck which appears to you.

In fact, your world is very much dependent on you. As your expression it is yours to explore, yours to learn from, yours to understand, yours to enjoy, yours to love, yours to make of it what you will.

Your world is a reflection of you.

~

At this preliminary stage it's certainly not necessary to understand every point; all will be explained during the course of the book. However, what I would like you to take away from this chapter is the idea that any world is much more than just a physical reality and you are much more than a conscious appearance.

Understanding the universe in terms of purely physical matter not only creates a misunderstanding as to the nature of matter (which is not so terrible) but creates a misunderstanding as to the nature of the world you experience, which is more significant as it can lead to unnecessary unhappiness in daily life.

However, the greatest misunderstanding this belief engenders relates to the understanding of what you are. Believing that your world is a collection of independent physical entities, you will assume that you also are something physical or, at least, an independent entity of some description. Believing that your world can be grasped conceptually you will believe that you can understand yourself conceptually.

This grave misunderstanding is the shadow in which all sense of incompleteness, imperfection, inadequacy and unfulfilled longing ferments.

~

You can think of your world in terms of physical matter, but I encourage you to also consider it in terms of perception arising from the sensation of consciousness. This is necessary if you are to make full sense of the world you experience.

Perceptions are the lifeblood of any world: they shape and differentiate it from all others. They are all you ever know and experience.

Without those perceptions there is no world ... and arguably not even a skerrick of matter.

5 It's a mental image

Let's turn our attention to some practical exercises.

While you might understand that your world appears as a product of consciousness, and reason that it exists as a mental image, if you are to properly understand this perspective it is important to actually experience the perspective for yourself.

While my experience of this perspective resulted from extended meditative practice, I hope to introduce you to the experience of this perspective through a fairly simple exercise. In order to get full value out of it, don't just read the words, do the exercise. You can't properly understand by just reading the words.

~

To do this exercise get yourself a drink and place it near you, make yourself comfortable and close your eyes.

To start, visualise the drink in as much detail as you can. Picture the shape and colour of the container and the appearance of the liquid. It may be a rather vague image but, nevertheless, it is a mental image.

Then once you have formed the mental image open your eyes and look at the drink. Notice the details that come into focus: the shape is clear, the colours are more vivid and the shades of light and shadow are a surprise. Observe the detail which was absent in the picture of your memory.

Now as you look at the drink, appreciate that it can still be perceived as a mental image. While the image is clearer and appears to be an object outside your head, it can, nevertheless, be recognised as an image appearing in your mind ... a mental image which now incorporates visual sensory information.

If you can experience this perspective you are well on your way to perceiving your world as a mental image.

—

Now that you are looking at the drink, imagine what it will feel like when you pick it up. Try to get as complete a mental image as you can.

Then when you've formed the image pick up the drink. Feel the container against your fingers and the palm of your hand. Notice aspects of the texture and temperature which you hadn't envisioned but which appear now that you have touched it.

Even though you are touching the drink, it still can be perceived as a mental image. The tactile sensations don't change the fact of the mental image ... they enhance it.

—

Now, while you are holding the drink, consider what it will taste like. Picture the taste as accurately as you can.

Once you have that image, sip your drink. Notice the sensation of the drink in your mouth. Focus on the taste, texture and temperature. Observe the aspects of taste which come into existence after you taste it.

The point that I'd like to make here is in the same vein as the previous points. Whereas the mental image was imbued with visual and tactile information, it is now imbued with the sensation of taste. The mental image is more complete than when you just held, looked at or imagined the drink; however, crucially, your entire experience can still be perceived as a mental image.

Everything you experience can be recognised as a mental image appearing in your mind.

~

The exercise is straight forward; you engage in many activities like this every day of your life. However, by paying more attention to what you are experiencing than you normally would, I hope that you have been able to experience a different perspective. I hope that you can appreciate that every aspect of the drink can exist – does exist – as a mental image to you.

If you are to understand what I am trying to share with you in this book, it is vital that you are able to experience this perspective for yourself.

At this stage you most likely believe that the mental images you experience are of a physical object. That is fine. However, as we work through the book I hope that you will come to realise that the mental images aren't of an object, but that the so-called 'objects' are actually mental images.

⁓

While the primary purpose of this chapter is to encourage you to perceive the common objects in your world as mental images, I would like to draw your attention to the role of sensations.

At each stage of the exercise mental images were shaped and refined by your sensations. With closed eyes the mental image was based on remembered sensations. With eyes open, the image became clearer. And when you drank the drink, additional dimensions were revealed. The more sensory information you gathered, the more detailed and rich the mental image became.

While the mental image was shaped by sensations (if you change the sensation, you change the mental image), the relationship between them is far more intricate than that. The mental image you experienced isn't of the relevant sensation ... the sensation is the mental image. There is no separation between the two ... sensations exist as mental images.

In this regard, it's important to remember that any mental image you experience is not a flat two-dimensional image, but rather a multi-dimensional, incredibly complex, rich and vibrant mental image comprising detailed sensory information, imbued with significance, meaning, intellect and emotion.

The mental image is the total experience of life ... not a copy of it, but the actual experience. It is your life.

~

Getting back to our exercise, yes it certainly was extremely simple, but I hope that it has demonstrated that:

- At all times the drink appears as a mental image in your mind

- The appearance of the mental image is determined by sensations

- The sensations appear as mental images, and

- The mental image is multi-dimensional and very complex.

Of course, these principles don't just apply to the drink but to everything that you experience. Every object and event, regardless of size, distance, age or significance can be perceived as a mental image ... including the world you experience.

~

Hopefully this exercise has been a useful introduction to a different way of perceiving your world.

I am aware that even if you can experience the mental image perspective that you may still harbour a strongly held view that, nevertheless, you are observing physical and independent objects which are at some core level tangible.

This is an eminently valid point that we shall turn our attention to in the next chapter.

6 It's all in your mind

I don't think that there is any real dispute that the world you observe appears as a mental image. If there is a dispute, it relates to what gives rise to the mental image.

On the one hand, you may want to argue that any mental image is due to the existence of a physical object ... so if the mental image of a tree forms in your mind you will say that you are looking at a physical tree.

On the other hand, the view I take is that the mental image is not due to a physical tree but to non-tangible sensory information which is interpreted by the brain as a seemingly physical tree. That image exists in the mind. Beyond the mind there is no physical tree.

In this chapter I'd like to explore this issue by investigating what we know about a seemingly physically object – such as a tree – to see if we can discover anything physical about it.

⁓

If you look at a tree you can describe its appearance. You can note details about the girth and texture of its trunk, the formations of its branches, and the colour and shape of its leaves.

The appearance of the tree will look like a physical object, however if you were successful with the previous exercise you will also be able to appreciate that this appearance can also be perceived as a mental image appearing in your mind.

Even if you were to touch the leaves, pull on a branch and slap the trunk, you will be able to appreciate that these sensations also form part of the mental image. Yes, the tree may seem like a physical object yet, nonetheless, your experience of it is as a mental image.

Actually, any sensory experience you can have about the tree can be understood as merely furnishing a more detailed mental image.

~

While it may appear that the tree is a physical object, I would suggest that this is not a fact but an untested assumption that needs to be investigated.

Although we can definitely state that we experience a mental image of the tree, we have no proof that there is an underlying physical tree which gives rise to the mental image.

Admittedly, that's not to say that underlying physical layers don't exist, but simply that if they do, then we need to undertake a more detailed investigation to uncover them.

So let's consider what scientific investigation can reveal about the underlying nature of the tree.

~

If we investigate the tree from a botanical perspective, we could identify its class and species; and reveal some interesting information about its evolutionary development and relationship to its environment and other trees. Could we consider this as proof of the existence of a physical object?

Or, if you wanted to dig a bit deeper you could analyse the biological structure of the tree and uncover underlying complex structures such as cells and tissues. Is this evidence of a physical structure?

Or, if you wanted to go further you could undertake a chemical analysis to determine the chemical composition of the tree, even to the extent of revealing its atomic configuration. Would this be proof that the tree is at heart a tangible object?

Or, perhaps you could go even further and trace the underlying metaphysics of the tree to abstruse ideas about particles, waves, quarks, strings and membranes. Would this uncover the physical reality of the tree?

With this detailed scientific analysis, have we uncovered a physical aspect of the tree: a reality which isn't a mental image?

~

It may be tempting to think so, but when you consider the matter in more detail you realise that despite all your research, you are still left with a mental image of the tree. Sure, the mental image is now significantly more detailed and your understanding is more comprehensive, yet still it is a mental image.

Regardless of how many layers of the tree are peeled back, you cannot discover anything which is conclusively not a mental image ... each layer is experienced as just another aspect of perception. And so despite the wealth of information you've gathered you are still dealing with the tree as a mental image. Insights are developed but no physical reality is discovered: it is only ever inferred.

~

So we are left with an interesting situation. Our intention was to discover something physical about the tree and yet after as detailed an exploration of the tree as scientific analysis will allow, we cannot find anything which is conclusively physical.

Actually, all we have uncovered are further mental images. We haven't discovered any aspect of the tree which can't be perceived as a mental image. Nor have we been able to disprove that what we are observing is a mental image. We haven't been able to prove that anything physical exists separate to the mental image. We haven't even been able to prove that anything physical exists.

Sure, we can agree that our investigations reveal incredible complexity. That is undeniable. However, any attempt to categorise this complexity as evidence of physicality or tangibility is, at best, an inference.

Everything we can know about this complexity is revealed to us as a mental image.

~

Admittedly, while our investigations don't conclusively disprove the existence of physical structures, at the very least they open up the question as to what is the nature of what we are observing.

I'd suggest that rather than start with the assumption that what we observe is tangible, it is far preferable to start with the observation that everything we perceive is a mental image. From that point we can then investigate the underlying structure to determine if it is physical, mental, neither physical nor mental, or both physical and mental.

At this early juncture of the book you don't need to come to a firm conclusion one way or the other; just be aware that the issue is open. Despite appearances, tangibility is not a given.

~

While I suggest that while the issue is open, it has remained stubbornly closed in mainstream thinking.

Rather than question the existence of physical structures, it has been commonly assumed that the world is unquestionably physical.

Perhaps one reason why this stubbornness remains is due to our use of language. When we use a word to name an object – star, rock, tree, atom – it creates the impression that we are naming a thing … a physical reality. However, we need to be open to the possibility that when we use a word we are actually naming a mental image.

While words are useful tools of communication, they may not be indicative of physicality.

~

From my perspective, I don't assume that any object is physical or mental. I simply observe. And when I observe … whether the beach made up of countless grains of sand, to the universe made up of countless atoms of star dust, to the dark emptiness of space which lies beyond … I recognise all as an incredible image appearing on the dimensionless screen of my mind.

No matter how familiar, intricate or beautiful it appears, I recognise that it exists as an interesting aspect of perception, made possible by consciousness.

In my view nothing is tangible. Nothing possesses the slightest solidity. All is conceptual in nature and, ultimately, formless and shapeless.

Only in appearance does anything seem tangible: that appearance, like a moving sun, is the illusion. Beneath that appearance lies the intangible reality.

⁓

Survival in a seemingly physical world doesn't require the inference of tangibility.

It merely requires the recognition that what is essentially intangible can present to you as tangible objects and physical realities.

Armed with that knowledge it's up to you to respond accordingly.

⁓

That's my perspective. And in sharing it, I am not in any way attempting to diminish the nature of the objects you perceive. Rather, I am attempting to place them in their correct context. In so doing I hope that it gives you greater insight into the role and reaches of mind.

It is my experience that this perspective is a crucial step to the ultimate realisation of what you are. The dogmatic assertion that physical realities do exist is an insurmountable obstacle.

7 All sensations are mental phenomena

It is interesting that, with just a minor shift of perspective, what originally appeared to be an external physical object can be perceived as a mental image. It's equally interesting to note that, with this shift, what appeared to be an independent object can be perceived as your personal experience.

You can scientifically investigate that object to determine if it is, in fact, physical, but in so doing you actually only realise a more detailed and complex mental image.

While, at this stage, we cannot categorically state that there is no physical aspect to what we perceive, we can certainly be confident that mental images exist at all conceivable levels of experience.

You may not be ready to conclude that there are no physical objects which exist beyond mind. That said, you may be starting to question some of your assumptions about the nature of physical objects, the depths of mind and the existence of a world as an objective reality.

In time you may come to see that the existence of an objective world is a myth: that mind is vast and encompasses the entire universe and that physical objects are actually mental phenomena appearing in mind, having no independent existence.

~

Of course you have every right to be skeptical. If I were in your situation I would be skeptical too. After all, what I am suggesting runs contrary to long established concepts about the nature of the world and, well, 'common sense'.

It is fine to be skeptical but please remain open minded as we continue our exploration of your world.

Instead of continuing our search for indisputably physical objects and particles – which might not even exist – let's approach the issue from a different angle. Let's consider what definitely exists as a mental image and cannot exist as a physical reality. In so doing we may glimpse what gives rise to the mental image.

~

Rather than focus on thoughts, beliefs, memories and feelings – which are clearly mental phenomena – I'd like to turn our attention to the tastes and smells, tactile sensations and visual appearances where there may be an element of doubt.

To help us frame our discussion, we'll use the example of an apple and will start with the sensation of taste.

When you look at an apple you might be tempted to think that taste is a physical property waiting to be experienced. However, that is not so. Taste only arises with the experience of tasting. Without that experience taste doesn't exist.

While the apple may have the potential for taste, that potential is not the same as the sensation of taste.

As such, before you take a bite of the apple, it has no taste. The taste only comes into existence after you have bitten it and experienced it as a sensation.

That sensation is an appearance in mind and only exists in mind.

Accordingly, taste is an entirely mental phenomenon. There is no taste beyond the mind.

~

While you may agree that taste only exists as a sensation, you may still want to assert that there are chemical compounds in the food which give rise to the sensation of taste and exist beyond the mind's mental image.

This is an excellent point which will be considered in chapter 9. At this stage we will focus on the aspects of apple which clearly exist as mental phenomena.

~

Having made the point that taste is a sensation which only exists in the mind, let's consider another couple of senses ... smell and touch.

Using the same logic, you could conclude that the apple of itself and by itself has no smell. It may have the potential for smell, but that potential isn't smell. Like taste, a smell only comes into existence through the act of smelling. Without the smelling there is no smell. An un-smelt smell isn't a smell.

It isn't difficult to conclude that smell is a sensation which only exists as a mental image.

With regard to the sense of touch, we could also conclude that the apple has no tactile sensation until it is touched. While we may be able to infer what the apple might feel like, that inference is not tactile sensation. Tactile sensation depends on the experience of touch. Without the experience there is no tactile sensation ... just the potential for it.

We can confidently state that tactile sensation is a sensation that only exists as a mental image.

⁓

Hopefully, we can agree that taste, smell and touch only exist as mental appearances, but how about a more challenging sense such as vision? Do the same principles apply to the visual appearance of an apple? Does its appearance only exist once seen?

In my view, yes it does. However, as this is a slightly more difficult point to grasp, let's run through the logic again.

If I close my eyes for a moment and then open them, the apple is there, immediately. If I close my eyes and open them again, the apple is still there.

The visual appearance of the apple is so instantaneous that I could easily assume that the visual appearance of the apple persists even when my eyes are closed. That is the illusion.

In actuality, just like the other senses, prior to looking at the apple it has no visual appearance. When I look at the apple its visual appearance comes into existence. When I close my eyes the visual image disappears. When I open my eyes again the visual image is recreated.

The trick here is to remember that we are talking about the visual appearance of the apple. That appearance does not exist independently of the experience of seeing, but only as a product of seeing. In the absence of seeing there is no visual appearance … just its potential.

Like our other sensory information, visual appearance arises as a sensation and only exists as a mental image.

~

So what does this tell me about the apple?

Well, any experience that I can have about the apple is a product of my sensations. Its visual appearance is determined by how it appears to me. Its tactile sense is a result of how it feels to me. Its smell is dependent on my olfactory senses and its taste only exists as my experience of it.

All these aspects of the apple exist as products of my senses. They are mental images which appear in my mind. The apple as I experience it exists in my mind.

Actually, the apple so completely exists in my mind that there is no demarcation where I can separate the apple from my perception of it. There is no point where my perception stops and the apple starts.

My perception isn't of the apple … the apple is my perception of it.

⏴

Furthermore, by virtue of a habit of thinking in terms of physical realities, I may want to infer the existence of the apple in the absence of my experience of it … however, all that I can confidently state is that there was the potential for the apple I subsequently experienced.

Through my experiences that potential was transformed into the apple which took shape and form in my mind. Its appearance was determined by my sensations, which were dependent on my consciousness.

⏴

This leads to an interesting question. What is the apple like in the absence of my mental images of the apple? What is the apple like in the absence of my sensory experiences? What is the apple like in the absence of my conscious awareness? What is an unperceived apple like?

You will need to ponder these questions, but we can make the following observations.

As the apple is untasted, it has no taste. As the apple is unsmelt, it has no scent. As the apple is untouched it has no tactile sensation. As the apple is unseen it has no visual appearance.

So what sort of apple are we dealing with?

It is an 'apple' which is shapeless and formless. It can't be said to be tangible. It has the potential to be the apple I recognise, but it certainly isn't that apple which appears in my mind's eye courtesy of my senses.

The only reason why I might assume that there is an actual apple – which exists independently of my sensory experiences – is due to my assumptions. I would suggest that this inference is a misunderstanding.

The apple I experience exists as the result of my experiences and requires those experiences to exist as it does. In the absence of those experiences, the apple I experienced can't be said to exist.

Yes, those experiences may create the appearance of tangibility but that appearance is an aspect of the mental image. Without the mental image there is no question of tangibility.

We could also note that the apple which arises from my experiences and exists as a mental image is dependent on my conscious awareness. Without that conscious awareness there is no experience, no mental image and no apple to speak of.

Instead, there is just the potential for the apple I subsequently experienced.

~

Of course, these principles are equally applicable to everything I experience in my world.

Whatever I experience depends on my conscious awareness; it comes into existence as a product of my senses and exists as mental phenomena.

In the absence of that mental image there isn't a murky object waiting to appear. Rather, there is the potential for any number of mental images.

That potential is devoid of all sensations. It is even devoid of conscious awareness.

~

I know that it is tempting to want to infer the existence of a pre-existing tangible world just like the mental image of the world we are familiar with. However, while it might be tempting ... can we even begin to imagine a world devoid of mental images, sensations and conscious awareness?

And can we really be so confident to presume that we know what exists in the absence of everything we know?

These issues require careful consideration.

~

We've used a practical example to demonstrate that sensations are mental phenomena. As mental images, they are aspects of mind and do not exist independently to mind.

What exists in the absence of sensory experiences is nothing like the sensory world you are familiar with. As unrealised potential, it is shapeless and formless. It isn't tangible. You can't even imagine it.

We will be considering the nature of this mysterious potential in greater detail and especially its relationship to mind and the experience of your world.

But before that, let's continue our exploration of what can only exist within the boundaries of the mind ... and in particular a world which is sensory, but not physical, in nature.

8 The power of perceiving

Zen Koans are traditional Japanese writings that are designed to push the mind beyond its conditioned way of thinking so that a more profound understanding can be realised.

I remember reading one of these Koans some years ago, which I am sure that you will also be familiar with ...

If a tree falls in the forest and no one is there to hear it, does it make a sound?

I recall being surprised by the question. It was my first exposure to a suggestion that something might not exist in the absence of experience.

While the riddle was designed to encourage a deeper consideration of the nature of reality, I admit that I didn't rise to the challenge.

As I toyed with the question I realised that it couldn't be answered through empirical observation, but instead of probing the issues raised by the riddle, I assumed that there would be a sound, regardless of whether someone was there or not. I reasoned that when the tree falls it produces sound waves which exist independently of the presence or absence of a person to hear them.

This conclusion reflected my belief that the world existed independently of me and certainly wasn't dependent on me.

I maintained that perspective for many years.

⌣

Since then, as you might have guessed, my understanding has changed. Even if, for the sake of argument, I concede that sound waves are generated when a tree falls, I now claim that sound waves aren't the same as sound. A sound wave is not sound.

Why do I say this? Well, consider the physics of sound.

When sound waves are channelled into an ear canal, vibrations occur on the ear drum, which are then relayed to and processed by the brain. The result is sound. Prior to this process there may be sound waves, but there is no sound. Sound only arises as a product of hearing.

Sound isn't what enters the ear canal. Sound is the result of auditory processes. Without an ear to hear, there is no sound.

So, with regards to the Koan, does a tree make a sound if no one is there to hear it? … the answer must be 'no'. Sound only arises when an ear is present to convert, through the process of hearing, sound waves into sound.

⌣

If you have any difficulty understanding this point, it will be because you assume that sound exists independently of the experience of sound.

What I hope to make very clear is that sound *is* the experience of sound. If there is no experience of sound, then there is no sound. This is a crucial point to grasp.

Of course, even if you agree that without an ear to hear there is no sound, you may want to pick me up on my concession that sound waves are generated when a tree falls. If so, you will want to claim that even if there is no sound that nevertheless there are sound waves which are physical realities that exist beyond the mental image. This is a good point, which we will consider in the next chapter.

⁓

For the time being though, I'd like to return to the line of thought raised by the Koan to ask another interesting question:

If a tree falls in the forest and a thousand creatures are there to hear it, does it make one sound or a thousand sounds?

While it might be tempting to claim that the falling tree makes just one sound, on reflection this assumption can't be correct.

If one creature is present, sound waves will be channelled into the ear drum and then processed by the brain, producing sound. So if one creature is present, one sound will exist.

If, however, one thousand creatures are present, then sound waves will be channelled into one thousand ear drums, producing not one sound but one thousand sounds.

There isn't one common sound shared by all the creatures, but one thousand different sounds.

～

Each of these thousand sounds exist as the particular creature experiences it. As no two experiences can be identical, no two sounds will be identical. Instead, each of those sounds is a unique manifestation … different from all others.

Because sound exists as an experience, the nature of those thousand sounds is determined by the sensory capacity of the creature experiencing it. In other words, each sound is a product of the particular ear/brain which hears it.

These sounds not only differ between differing species such as humans, birds, bears, dogs and snakes, but also between the same species. No two dogs hear the exact same sound, nor do two humans.

～

If there is no instrument to hear, then there can be no sound. Without an ear, the universe is absolutely silent … that silence cannot even be recognised.

Only when there is an instrument to hear can sound and silence come into existence. Both sound and silence exist as a product of the hearing.

Once heard, sound exists as it is experienced. It varies from species to species and creature to creature. It is a multifaceted, infinitely nuanced phenomenon.

As such, sound is not an objective reality. It is a subjective experience. It only exists in the mind of the hearer.

Without that subjective experience, there is no sound … just the potential for innumerable manifestations of sound.

An unheard sound is not sound … at best it is the potential for sound.

⁓

It's difficult for me to gauge how you will find this chapter. Maybe you will find it novel, maybe interesting, maybe obvious, maybe challenging.

The message that I want you to take away from this chapter is that, like all sensations, sound is a personal experience. It exists as a product of mental processes. It exists in the mind of the experiencer. And it is not an objective reality.

When those one thousand creatures hear sound, they are not hearing the one sound. They hear a sound which is unique to them … or more correctly, they manifest a sound which is unique to them.

Because the act of hearing is the act of manifesting sound, there can be no one sound common to all. Rather, sound exists as a thousand different experiences. It is those different experiences.

In the absence of hearing, there is just the potential for sound.

9 Cause and effect are mental images

In the last chapter it was suggested that sound exists as an experience and that there is no underlying sound separate to its experience.

This principle doesn't just apply to sound (or taste, smell, touch or visual appearance). Instead I would encourage you to apply it to anything that can be perceived. Whatever you perceive – whether object, event or imagination – exists as your experience of it. Every experience exists as a mental image.

As demonstrated by the sound example, whatever mental image you form is not the only interpretation. There are an infinite number of other perspectives, resulting from diverse sensory and intellectual capacities, which vary greatly in appearance and detail.

These perspectives don't just exist in the minds of human beings, but also in the minds of various animals and insects. And while we may not think of plants as having minds and perspective, they do experience and react to 'sensations' which are reflected in, say, a gnarled trunk, leaves fluttering in the breeze or a tree falling in the forest. Even non-organic matter, such as rocks, elements and atoms, has its own perspective which can be observed through the transference of energy and a range of chemical reactions.

At every conceivable level there is perceiving in accordance with the capacity to perceive.

~

If there is a consensus in our considerations to date it is that our respective personal worlds exist as mental phenomena. We might also agree that these worlds are contingent upon consciousness and are shaped by sensations.

What may possibly remain in dispute is the issue of just what gives rise to these mental worlds. Is there a tangible reality which underpins all subjective worlds – your world being one interpretation of this tangible reality? Or does no such tangible reality exist? Does all have the substance of non-tangible potential?

While the 'tangible reality' view may seem reasonable, there are difficulties with it, not the least of which being that its existence can't be proved. Even when an intensive search for this tangible reality is undertaken, we expose a more detailed and complex mental image but can't claim discovery of anything tangible or even separate to that mental image.

In contrast, the 'no tangible reality' view would appear to be supported by the evidence considered to date, but may be resisted if there is a strong belief that there must be something tangible underpinning any mental appearance.

We are left with the choice between sticking with our beliefs as to the existence of a tangible reality (which we cannot prove exists) or, alternatively, accepting that there is no such tangible reality (even though we may have trouble believing it). This presents an interesting dilemma.

I'd like to attempt to resolve this seeming impasse by teasing out the thinking behind the two approaches. Hopefully, the discussion won't be too complicated.

～

If you are persuaded that there is a tangible reality, then you will think that there must be a tangible cause underpinning any mental image you experience. As such, in the case of sound and taste we recently considered, you will reason that sound is caused by sound waves and taste is caused by chemical compounds in the food. You will claim that these aren't mental phenomena and do exist beyond the scope of mind.

Although this line of reasoning might seem fairly convincing, the 'no tangible reality' perspective views this approach as flawed as it doesn't appreciate the nature of the 'cause' that has been identified.

While you might think that you have identified a cause, what you have actually done is develop a conceptual interpretation of the cause. That conceptual interpretation – whether 'sound wave' or 'chemical compound' – may be well researched, may be verifiable experimentally and may even, broadly speaking, be accurate ... but, nevertheless, as an interpretation it is a conceptual understanding ... an idea.

As such rather than identify a cause that exists beyond the mind, what you have done is identify a 'cause' which actually exists as a mental image in your mind. In fact, the mental image of the cause is no different from the other mental images it tries to explain.

The conclusion is that not only are sound and taste mental phenomena, but so too are any explanations about how those sensations arise ... regardless of how convincing they may seem. These explanations may attempt to make greater sense of the world you experience, yet, nevertheless, they are just mental contrivances that do not exist beyond the conscious mind.

Significantly, as mental contrivances, they aren't the actual cause ... any more than the idea of pain is pain, or the idea of consciousness is consciousness, or the idea of an unperceived 'object' is an unperceived 'object'.

The mental image of the sound wave isn't the actual cause of sound and the mental image of chemical compounds isn't the actual cause of taste. They may happen to be faithful approximations, but as conceptual interpretations they fail to grasp the actual reality.

They are an idea about the cause, but they aren't the cause. They are an interpretation of the reality, but aren't the reality. They are the map, but not the territory.

~

Crucially, this principle doesn't just apply to sound waves or chemical compounds, but extends across absolutely every conceptual explanation that can be formed. Concepts of 'big bang' and quantum mechanics, subatomic particles and atoms, physical laws and chemical properties, physical objects and conscious perception are all conceptual interpretations. They are mental images which exist in the mind, but they do not capture the actual cause.

The reason why these sorts of mental images don't capture the underlying cause is because the underlying cause isn't a mental image (whether idea, explanation, description, interpretation or understanding) and can't be understood as such. The actual cause can't be squeezed into a conceptual formulation. That reality is beyond conceptual thinking.

Of course this does raise an intriguing question: if the concept 'sound wave', the concept 'chemical compound' and the concept of anything else is not the cause of sound, taste or anything else, what then is that actual cause of the mental images which populate our respective worlds?

We will turn our attention to this very important question over the next few chapters.

10 The shape of mind

Your world may be filled with sights and sounds, colours and shapes, but no matter how vast, ancient or infinitely varied it may seem it arises as a product of consciousness; it is shaped by sensations and exists as a mental image appearing in your mind.

No matter how far you traverse this world in space or time, or how deeply you explore its most mysterious recesses you cannot discover anything which exists as a tangible entity.

Despite your sharpest intellect or most determined efforts, you cannot uncover anything which is not a mental image. Succeeding layers of mental appearance are revealed, but no physical essence. Nothing exists beyond the scope of mind; even concepts of space and time are revealed as mere mental projections.

You can ascribe explanations in an attempt to gain some understanding about the nature of your world – how it came to appear, and why it functions as it does – but all those explanations are conceptual interpretations, amounting to nothing more than mental images.

No matter how hard you try with your intellect you cannot scratch beneath the surface of the mental image to gain any depth of understanding beyond the mental image. Any explanation, whether 'sound wave', 'chemical compound', 'atom' or 'energy' is a conceptual interpretation, but not the actual reality.

That reality which lies beyond those mental images is neither a tangible reality nor a mental image. It is more like potential.

⁓

So let's apply this theory to a practical setting. Let's consider the situation where we are looking at a stone.

The stone will appear to you as a mental image in your mind. That mental image comes into existence as a product of perceiving and is unique to you. Similarly, that stone will also appear to me as a unique mental image. Armed with our respective, but different, mental images we would no doubt be happy to agree that we are looking at a stone.

If we vary the example slightly so that you didn't perceive the stone but I did, then we would be in the situation where your mental image of the stone wouldn't exist, but my mental image would. If I told you about the stone, you could, based on that description, form a mental image of the stone. However, in the absence of that description you would have no mental image of the stone and it wouldn't exist to you. It would, however, exist to me.

If we tweak the example a little more so that neither of us perceived the stone, then we would be in a situation where neither of us would have a mental image of the stone and it wouldn't exist to us.

This leaves us with an interesting question ... if neither of us have a mental image of the stone, does the stone exist?

This is a challenging question. We could answer that as our perceptions of the stone don't exist, then what does exist is the unperceived 'stone'. This unperceived 'stone' isn't anything like the stone we perceive; instead it is the 'stone' without our perceptions. To understand what this might be like you need to consider the stone without all your mental images, without all your senses and without your conscious awareness. In other words, you would need to appreciate the 'stone' from the perspective of the 'stone'. Devoid of vision, intellect and, indeed, consciousness that perspective would be nothing like your or my perception.

If you want to understand the 'stone' in this raw 'unperceived' state, you will have challenges. Without the aid of consciousness that state is incomprehensible, but as soon as you employ consciousness that raw state is lost. Actually, this raw state defies all conceptual understanding and is beyond any intellectual framework.

That said, we can make some comments about this unperceived state.

With the benefit of consciousness we can observe that this raw state does exist and we might even be able to describe it as potential. It is the potential which is subsequently expressed as mental images in our respective minds. As such, we might be able to say that the potential exists as a range of possibilities. Those possibilities – one of which is the appearance of tangibility – are only realised when the 'stone' is perceived ... by me, you, or someone or something else.

If the stone isn't perceived by us, its potential could, nevertheless, be 'perceived' at chemical and atomic levels. Of course, those 'perceptions' are nothing like our respective conscious perceptions, but nonetheless they could be said to exist.

That said, if there is absolutely no perception at any level, then there is absolutely no stone. All that we can say is that there is pure potential which is absolutely unrealised. Furthermore, any concept we form about that potential, it is not that.

~

We will consider this unperceived state in greater detail when we turn our attention to the nature of reality; however, at this stage let's continue our exploration of what, through the filter of consciousness, we do perceive.

Having formed the mental image of a stone we can investigate it to determine its type (igneous, sedimentary or metamorphic), its particular constituent elements, and the processes that led to its formation.

We can also observe that at every stage of development perception was a vital ingredient.

While we don't usually think of perception operating at non-conscious levels, nevertheless, at a sub-atomic level a primordial type of perception was necessary for atoms to form, at an atomic level a similar perceptive ability was necessary for chemicals to bond, and at a geological level a rudimentary perception was necessary for those chemical bonds to react to various geological forces.

In addition, conscious perception was necessary for the appearance of the stone as it appears to you or me, and indeed for the various investigations we undertook.

We could say that every aspect of the perceived stone is a product of perceiving. In the absence of that perceiving the necessary interactions and crucial stages of development would not have been possible.

Without multiple levels of perceiving at both non-conscious and conscious levels, the appearance of a seemingly tangible stone in your or my mind could not have arisen.

~

While there may be the strong sense that there must be a tangible reality underpinning the appearance of the stone – presumably a sub-atomic particle, atom or element – there is another view which maintains that the appearance of the stone isn't due to tangible phenomena, but rather non-tangible phenomena.

According to this view, even though the mental image of the stone seems tangible, actually there is no tangible core. Instead it is an illusion resulting from infinite levels of perceiving ... perceiving at the sub-atomic level leading to perceiving at the atomic level leading to perceiving at the conscious level.

The resulting appearance of the seemingly tangible stone results from a history of perceiving. That perceiving may encompass the length, breadth and history of the universe, yet no underlying tangible object is involved.

I would suggest that the reason why there is no underlying tangibility is because what is perceived is not a tangible core particle but, instead, pure potential ... the very essence of the universe.

⌒

I am aware that there may be great reluctance to abandon the idea that there is a tangible reality which underpins the existence of the seemingly tangible and real world you are familiar with; however, the problem with this view is that there is no such tangible object.

Take water, for example. When you observe water it appears to have a number of unique and highly significant physical properties, which make it an undeniably tangible phenomenon. However, when you investigate the water, it is revealed to be a combination of hydrogen and oxygen. On further examination these elements are found to exist as atoms, which in turn are revealed to be space-like sub-atomic particles. Ultimately, under further scrutiny even these seemingly fundamental building blocks aren't tangible objects, but theoretical conceptualisations appearing in the minds of quantum physicists trying to work out what lies at the heart of what they are observing.

At every stage – water, chemical, atom, sub-atomic particle – it appears that you uncover a tangible object but what you actually reveal are more intricate, and indeed fundamental, levels of perception.

There is no core that you can identify as tangible real water.

Why? Well, arguably because it doesn't exist as a tangible phenomenon.

Instead, all you can identify are multiple levels of perceiving, which result in your perception of water ... and ultimately point to the infinite potential which is its source.

～

And here's the paradox. While the water you observe is a mental appearance, existing as the perceiving of it ... if you fall in the water you get wet, and if you don't drink it, your body cannot survive.

This tells us that the act of perceiving, at both non-conscious and conscious levels, plays a crucial role in shaping the appearance and parameters of your world and all other worlds.

Perceiving transforms the potential into everything ... sub-atomic particles, atoms, elements ... water, stone ... life forms, your body/mind ... and a host of other mental objects. It all seems tangible but all is an appearance made possible by perceiving.

Without perceiving there can be no perception.

Once you come to the realisation that *everything* that you can be conscious of exists as a mental image made possible by perceiving, then you will be ready to glimpse what lies beyond.

11 Perception changes Everything

Just as there is nothing tangible in your world, there is nothing tangible in any world. All worlds are mental in nature.

These worlds exist simultaneously, and while each world is unique, they can't be separated from each other. One is intrinsic to all others.

Although they are infinite in number, together they comprise the one indivisible universe.

There is no solid core to this universe. It is entirely conceptual.

—

This notion of an entirely abstract universe is a tantalising prospect but it does raise further questions.

If your world isn't comprised of tangible objects or events, why does it appear as it does? Why does it take the appearance of a particular set of shapes and colours? And why does it appear to be filled with so much diversity?

What's more, if your world is just a mental appearance existing in your mind, why does the world you experience seem fairly similar to the world I experience?

Why is it that we seem to share a common world? And if this world is mental in nature, why does it seem to be tangible?

Of course in order to address these questions I am going to have to rely on conceptual interpretations, which adopt words such as atoms and genetics. These words should be appreciated as vehicles of communication and not indicative of the existence of physical structures. Instead, they represent ideas which by their nature cannot capture the actual reality.

The actual reality is beyond all concepts.

—

With this rider in mind, let's consider the role of perception.

Perception is an expression of awareness and represents the recognition and interpretation of information. At a conscious level, perception results in the image that exists in your mind at any given moment. It could even be said to be that image.

So, why do you perceive as you do?

I would suggest that the reason is a consequence of history. When I use the word 'history, I am not just referring to the experiences which have shaped your perception since birth – the cultural and social conditioning you have embraced, the assumptions you have taken to be true, the likes and dislikes you have formed – but more significantly, your complete evolutionary development encompassing the entire history of mind and matter leading to this moment.

It is because of the convergence of this entire history that you have a body, experience consciousness, perceive sensory information and interpret it in the way you do. The entire history results in the appearance of a world you are familiar with … your perception.

This perception is unique to you and is a product of your unique history. Certainly, if any aspect of that history were different then the perception you currently enjoy would also be different. Conceivably, it could be so different that the world you experience would be unrecognisable from the world you are familiar with today.

～

Consider how different your world would appear if your evolutionary development had equipped you with the olfactory sense of a bear or the visual acuity of an eagle.

Then again, consider yourself with additional senses beyond the normal experience … senses that you can't even imagine. Or what if on your long history you were not equipped with the sense of, say, touch, or if the atoms which comprise your body were organised in such a way that consciousness didn't form part of your makeup.

In these cases your world would take on different dimensions that you cannot even begin to comprehend.

A simple fluke of evolutionary development not only determines which sensations are sensed, but if they are sensed at all. It not only determines how or what you perceive but if you perceive.

The result of your history is the appearance of a world with which you are intimately familiar. However, a simple deviation in any aspect of that history could completely alter that appearance.

Your world could be transformed into something radically different, totally unrecognisable and deeply foreign. Seemingly tangible objects could be changed beyond all recognition: they may not appear tangible; they may not appear as objects.

Perception alone has that power.

～

Using this logic, it should follow that a world that is experienced by a human is qualitatively different to a world experienced by an animal, precisely because of the differences in perception. These differences are a result of the history reflected in differing genetic structures, sensory capabilities and neural complexity.

The perception of the human will reveal a certain kind of world. The perception of an animal will reveal another.

The perception of a non-conscious organism or a highly advanced alien life form will reveal a very different kind of world ... perhaps unimaginably so.

Regardless of what world is revealed – whether of animal, insect, plant, bacterium or alien life-form – it is always explainable as the result of a particular history leading to a particular perception.

～

History not only determines whether worlds are perceived differently, but if they are perceived similarly.

As such, the seeming similarity of my world, your world or any other human world is arguably not due to the existence of a tangible world made up of a variety of tangible objects, but rather the similarity of human perception.

As such, the reason why human perception is so similar may be attributable to the fact that the vast majority of our ancestral history is identical. As a result of that common history, humans share very similar atomic structure, genetic composition, sensory capacity and neural functioning.

This shared history translates into perceptions which are very similar; so similar that you can relate to the world I describe and I can relate to the world that you describe. Indeed, they are so similar they create the illusion of a shared independently existing common world.

However, while our perceptions may be similar – extremely similar – they are not identical. And while our histories are similar they are not the same.

As such, your history which is unique to you results in your perception and my history which is unique to me results in my perception. Consequently, while the resulting perceptions are similar, perhaps very similar, they are actually unique, different and not the same.

What makes our worlds similar are similarities in perception. What makes them different are differences in perception.

⁓

I suggest that perception and its associated history can explain why anything appears as it does. There is no need to invoke the existence of a tangible reality underpinning that appearance.

Indeed, by changing perception everything about that appearance can change.

⁓

Although the world you enjoy or endure may seem to be the same world as experienced by everyone else ... as the natural expression of your perception, it is your personal and unique experience.

The unique history leading to your perception results in the unique mental image which is your world. Without that history the world you know doesn't exist. With that history it exists but only for you.

~

It certainly is interesting to consider your world in terms of perception. It is a crucial aspect of the perspective that I am trying to share.

Having considered the issue of perception, this now brings us to the burning question ... what is being perceived? What are these seemingly tangible objects around us? If there is no underlying tangible structure, what is there?

These highly significant questions will be addressed in the next chapter.

12 The depths of mind

The history of your perception may explain why you perceive as you do and why your perception is similar to other human beings, but the question "what is actually perceived?" remains unanswered.

Yes, you have perceptions, but what are you perceiving? If it is not tangible matter, then what is it? Yes, you can perceive change, but what is the stimulus for that changing appearance? Why can things change without any input from you?

And if your perceptions are supposedly just mental phenomena, why is it that you cannot exercise control over these mental phenomena? Why can't you stop unpleasant situations arising? Why is it that you can be shocked, astounded and deeply hurt by perceptions which are creations of your mind?

There is the sense that the action which governs your world does not exist at the level of your conscious perception, but beyond. After all, much of what happens during the course of your life is greater than what you could ever have imagined, let alone expected.

Indeed, what determines the type of life you live?

⌣

To help frame the issue, let's consider the most poignant example that I can think of ... the moment of death.

You receive a telephone call informing you that your loved one has been injured and that you need to go to the hospital. You arrive at the hospital just in time to be with your loved one during the last moments of their life. Even as you hold their hand, their life drains away, leaving you touching a lifeless body. You are left numb, shocked and in disbelief. This totally unexpected experience is beyond anything that you could have imagined when you woke up that morning. Your life is changed forever.

Can this distressing experience just be a product of perception?

In one sense, the answer must be 'yes'. As challenging as it may be, we can agree that those experiences on this sad day exist as your perception. Both the painful images of your dying loved one and the deep emotions you experienced are perceptions which exist in your mind. Without those particular perceptions, those experiences wouldn't occur.

And we can explain your ability to perceive these perceptions by reference to the particular history of your body and mind. However, while this history may explain why you can experience these perceptions and why you can be aware of change, it doesn't explain what is actually changing.

Can it really be your mere perceptions which cause your loved one to lose their life? In my view, clearly not!

⁓

What then is it that creates our life experiences?

Certainly, that 'something' which causes them is beyond your control. It can manifest situations which are totally unexpected, completely unwelcome and can shake you to the core. Whatever that 'something' is, you have no conscious awareness of it. It seems to be something external to you, maybe like fate, but it is elusive and difficult to identify.

What is this mysterious factor in our lives? What is the action which drives our changing perceptions?

In this chapter I will attempt to answer these questions and tackle the existence of seemingly independent action separate to perception. However, in order to do so, rather than invoke the existence of independent tangible phenomena I will seek to reappraise the scope and depth of mind.

I hope that my explanation is not too complicated.

⁓

I guess that when you consider your mind, you think of it as an entirely personal phenomenon, consisting of conscious thoughts and feelings. That is certainly true;

however, I would like to suggest that your mind is far more expansive than that.

After all, your mind not only includes those conscious aspects which are well known to you, but also extends its subconscious reaches to the mysteries which give rise to the peculiar quirks of your individual psyche.

That said, your mind doesn't stop there.

Beyond those conscious and sub-conscious aspects, there are so-called non-conscious aspects of mind which are deep and profound. While those roots are non-conscious, they are aware and incorporate the entire history of your mind. They extend to the very formation of a conceptual, and seemingly tangible, universe.

～

In the last chapter we noted that any perception you may have is the result and expression of your entire history.

I would make the comment that this history is encapsulated in the development of your mind ... it is reflected in the depths of your non-conscious mind, the habits of your subconscious mind, and the limitation of your conscious mind. The cumulative effect is that your mind generates thoughts, feelings, ideas and perceptions, and is the receptacle of knowledge and memories.

As such, if we were to trace the journey of any perception, its beginnings would stir in the depths of the non-conscious mind and ultimately be expressed as conscious perception. In other words, action occurs at the non-conscious depths and results in the subsequent emergence of perceptions which take shape as mental images.

In fact, the bulk of the work of the mind occurs at non-conscious levels. The resultant appearance of conscious perception represents just the tip of the iceberg. While this perception is crucial to the world you are familiar with, it is only surface. The underlying functioning is deep and non-conscious.

For this reason, although your world is your perception, it may, nevertheless, shock, astound and surprise you. You can't control it at the conscious level because the bulk of the action occurs at the non-conscious level. And because of the complex functioning at these depths, the resulting mental image is a multidimensional marvel appearing as a seemingly tangible world existing within the constraints of predictable physical laws.

Your sense that 'something' must give rise to the many and diverse mental images you observe is correct. However, that something is not tangible phenomena but the deeper workings of your mind.

The history of those workings not only gives structure and certainty to the world with which you are familiar, but also manifests the unanticipated and unexpected.

～

Your mind is even more incredible. It's depths are not only vast, but its reach is universal in implication.

This must be a puzzling claim if you have assumed that your mind is personal to you and separate from other minds. However, as I hope to demonstrate in the following example, your mind is not an individual phenomenon.

If we are talking and exchanging thoughts, you could assume that we both possess individual minds. However, as we interact and share ideas, the question then arises just where is the boundary between our respective individual minds? Just where does your mind start and where does it end? Where does my mind start and where does it end?

Your mind has influenced my mind and my mind has influenced yours ... irrevocably. It is not possible to undo this exchange of information. Given this cross-fertilisation, is there any way to identify your or my mind, or separate our respective minds one from the other? Indeed is there any separation?

I'd suggest that it is not possible to identify such a boundary for the simple reason that it doesn't exist. Further, if there is no border separating our individual minds then it could readily be argued that our minds are not separate and never have been.

~

Continuing with this line of thought, if there is no separation between our minds, this raises the question whether we are actually dealing with two independent minds at all. It may be that, rather than two minds, we are dealing with two aspects of the one mind. As such, despite the seeming individuality of our conscious minds, they may actually be expressions of the one underlying mind.

If this is the case, the deep reaches of your mind are not only the deep reaches of my mind but, indeed, all minds. All conscious minds are aspects of the one mind … the one mind without borders.

The action which stirs in those deep reaches not only results in the array of images which appear in your mind but all other seemingly independent minds.

That one mind produces the appearance of an infinite number of unique, divergent and even contradictory expressions which comprise countless numbers of worlds.

—

The variety, depth and nuance of the images are indicative of the virtually incomprehensibly complex activity of the depths of mind.

Multiple levels of activity in the mind result in the appearance of a complex world: a world which on one hand appears solid, yet is constantly changing; a world which seems to exist independently of you, but depends on you; a world which you appear to share, yet exists as your private experience; a world which appears to be tangible, but is actually mental; a world of marvel, beauty, order, coincidence and surprise; a world of thoughts and emotions, memories and imagination.

This one mind doesn't just achieve this for the world you are conscious of ... but a countless number of worlds.

And inasmuch as this one mind is indisputably your mind, whatever is perceived in your world – whether 'mental' or 'physical' – is an expression of your mind.

Every aspect of your world is a product of your mind ... the one mind.

⁓

The theory may be novel and possibly challenging, but what does it tell us about our initial example?

Yes, your experience of that traumatic situation exists as perceptions arising in the conscious aspects of mind. Without those perceptions, that situation could not exist as you perceive it.

However, those conscious aspects of mind don't control the situation; they interpret what becomes the situation. The true action which determines the fate of your loved one and the reaction you experience occurs at the level of the non-conscious aspects of mind.

Significantly, there is nothing about that whole experience which is in any way separate to your mind.

All is an appearance in mind. All is an expression of mind ... your mind ... the one mind.

⁓

Believing that any event, appearance or happening has its source as a tangible, non-mental phenomenon beyond mind is to fail to appreciate the breadth and depth of mind.

Despite contrary appearances, the individual mind is actually universal.

Assuming that the mind is a separate and discrete phenomenon will cause no end of confusion.

Your mind is vast. It encompasses everything.

When you view your world, you view your mind. When you explore your world, you explore your mind. And when you understand your world, you understand your mind.

13 Your waking dream

In my day to day life I am acutely aware that everything I perceive exists in my mind.

The predictability of physical structures, the unexpected twists and turns of fate and the idiosyncrasies of individual thoughts and feeling are recognised as expressions of my non-conscious mind.

Images of a seemingly real and vibrant world pass across the surface of my mind, but I am in no doubt that they are without depth or substance. The objects have no tangibility and the experiences exist as memories.

All is a product of my mind. It exists as my perception and depends on my consciousness. Nothing is independent of mind.

～

Over the last few chapters I have been sharing my perspective which leads me to the conclusion that my world, your world and indeed all other worlds are mental phenomena and not tangible realities.

I have arrived at this perspective as a result of direct experience arising from self-realisation and not as a result of reading words, concepts or formulated arguments on a page. As such, it would not be surprising if, at this stage, you are not wholly convinced that your world is a mental phenomenon and not a tangible reality. Hopefully this will change as we progress.

To date we have been working on developing an intellectual understanding to help clear some of the obstacles created by misunderstanding. I recognise that this alone is not sufficient and so the book will shift its focus, later on, to more practical matters, which should allow you to realise this perspective directly for yourself.

That said, from this point onwards I will not give any ground to the idea that tangible entities exist. Instead I will proceed on the basis that your world, my world and all other worlds are mental phenomena and intangible in nature.

⌒

Having disposed of tangible matter, this leads us to an interesting question ... what is the nature of a world which appears and exists in mind?

I guess that the first point to note is that if your world is not tangible, then it is intangible. That means that it is without substance. It is not a solid phenomenon.

Instead, a world which is in essence intangible exists as a collection of mental phenomena. Those phenomena may possess great diversity, yet in essence they are just mental images. They are products of mind.

I guess that if I were to liken a non-tangible world to anything, I would say that it bears a striking similarity to a dream. A dream, of course, is a non-tangible phenomenon and exists as a collection of mental images.

⁓

I know that people may not take all that much interest in their dreams and may not even remember them clearly, but take a moment to think about those nightly images which fill your mind during sleep.

When you dream, a variety of shapes and colours appear in your mind which you interpret as a range of things, people and situations.

- The objects in your dreams are virtually indistinguishable to objects in your waking life. You can touch and handle them, and they seem tangible and solid. Yet they are just appearances in your mind.

- The people seem like the people you meet while awake. They have their personalities and you can talk to and interact with them. Yet they are only dreamed images.

- The situations you encounter seem just as real as your waking reality. Whatever transpires in your dream – whether the worst tragedy or the greatest windfall – you believe with complete earnestness that it is actually happening. Your dreams are so convincing that even if they differ from your waking life you happily accept all without hesitation. Yet none of it is real, it is only a dream.

- You are conscious and can think and feel just as you do when you are awake. You can even experience happiness, love, fear and pain. Yet all are dreamed feelings and sensations.

You appear to have the same body and mind, and be the same person as when you are awake. However, that person is just a dreamed figure appearing in the dream. It is a mental appearance.

Your dreams can seem incredibly vivid and real – just as vivid and real as your waking world – yet they are only mental images forming part of a dream. There is nothing tangible about them. Anything that appears in the dream is just dream.

~

While you may not have considered it before, the daily world you experience is very similar to a dream.

Just like your dreams, your world is filled with incredible diversity, including seemingly tangible objects, unique individuals and compelling situations. It all seems tangible, yet none of it is. Instead, all exists as a succession of non-tangible mental images appearing in your mind.

Your world may appear to be vast, beautiful, incredible, terrible, but like a dream it is just a picture. Mental, it appears to be physical. Intangible, it appears to be tangible. Illusory, it appears to be real.

You may be convinced by the seeming universality of the mental image, yet every moment exists as your private experience and every experience exists as your perception of it.

Actually, your world is so dreamlike that it could easily be described as a dream ... your waking dream.

~

Of course, while you are dreaming in your sleep, it can be very difficult to recognise that what you dream is in fact a dream ... even when the impossible happens. Instead, you will tacitly accept that your dream world is not only plausible but tangible and real.

It is only on waking from the dream that you can appreciate the dream as dream. You can then come to the conclusion that everything that appeared in the dream – whether object, person or experience – existed as a series of mental images and that none of it was tangible or real.

Without waking you might have continued believing that the dream was real ... indefinitely.

~

Similarly, while you are caught up in your waking world it can be very difficult to appreciate that your world is also dream-like. Instead, you will continue to believe that your world is tangible and real.

Only by 'waking' to your waking dream can you appreciate it as such and see it in its correct perspective as dream-like.

~

I would like to encourage you to see your world in its correct perspective.

As you read these words, realise that this experience is playing out in your mind. The words, the meaning of the words, the book, the sensation of the book, are just mental images appearing in your mind. Realise that perspective.

As you look around recognise the familiar objects you see as appearances in mind. Remind yourself constantly that nothing you experience has any reality beyond the mind. Perceive all in its correct perspective.

As you consider the last 10 years of your life, realise just how very dreamlike it seems. And remember that this very moment is also just another dreamlike moment similar to the rest.

Never forget that your world is your waking dream.

~

Of course, you don't have to share this perspective. You can believe that your world is more than a mental image appearing in your mind.

That's entirely a matter for you.

I would, however, suggest that refusing to accept your world as a mental image is like refusing to accept that a dream is in fact a dream. The real problem is that you haven't woken up yet and can't see it in its correct perspective.

~

From my experience, the appreciation that your world is a mental phenomenon is an essential step on the path to self-realisation. It also happens to be the perspective that follows self-realisation.

~

Realise your world as dreamlike and you're on the way to waking up.

14 It seems real but is it the Reality?

Even if you can appreciate the logic that your world is a mental image, you may still be loath to categorise it as dream-like. After all, while there may be similarities between a dream and your world, they are not the same.

For one thing, while your world is subject to the laws of nature, a dream is not. In a dream the impossible is commonplace, whereas, although the rare or unusual may happen in your world, the impossible does not. There is a structure and order that is integral to your world which isn't essential to a dream.

For this reason, there is a tendency to distinguish your world from a dream. You will want to claim that while a dream may seem real, your world – even if it is your waking dream – is real.

⁓

In this chapter I don't want to pursue the line of thought that your world is a dream, but I do want to consider what we mean by the word 'real'.

When we refer to an object as real or an event as really happening, we signify a special quality that marks it as different from a dreamed object or event. But what is this special quality?

When we say something is real, what do we actually mean by that word? What makes anything in your world real? Indeed, how can anything be real if all is a mental image?

In trying to understand what is 'real', we will first consider commonly held assumptions about what it means for something to be real and then the inadequacy of these assumptions.

~

I think that the first point to note is that the most common understanding is that 'reality is what is sensed or experienced'. As such, there is a tendency to contrast these real experiences against something that is imagined. If something is real it is not imagined; not invented; not make-believe; not a dream; not fictitious. It is something that is sensed or experienced, and actually exists.

To apply this definition to some practical situations, we would say that a chair we sit on is real, whereas a make-believe chair we imagine is not real. Similarly, if we had a dream about a chair, we would say that while the dream was real, the chair in the dream wasn't real.

If we recall a childhood toy that we hadn't seen for years, we will claim that it was real even though it no longer exists. And if someone else tells us about their toy, we will believe that it was real even though it no longer exists and even though we never saw it.

We are happy to label all these objects as real because they are based on experience. Either they can be (or were) experienced, and can (or could) be verified by other people. Crucially, they are not pure imagination.

~

While this understanding is useful for many day to day situations, it is not satisfactory in all circumstances. Take, for example, mirages and illusions.

If you experience an illusion – say pools of water lying on a hot road – you can say that the visual experience of water really happened, but you cannot say that the water is real. Although the appearance of water is experienced and does seem real, that appearance is actually just a trick of the mind.

In this regard, the fact that what you sense and experience can seem real without actually being real demonstrates that what is sensed or experienced is not necessarily a reliable determinant of reality.

~

Indeed, the very fact that illusions and mirages exist forces us to ask some probing questions about what we think of as real.

If what you experience might not necessarily be real, how can you determine reality from the mere appearance of reality?

If your experience isn't a reliable guide, can you safely assume that anything you experience is real? Or, like an illusion, does everything you experience merely appear real?

~

These are certainly challenging questions, but before we attempt to answer them, allow me to make two observations.

Firstly, if what you experience is real, then that sense of reality is due to your sensory perception. Anything that you experience seems real because you can see, touch or in some way experience it ... or previously have seen, touched or experienced it. Conversely, without a sensory experience of some kind, the sense (as opposed to belief) that something is real doesn't arise.

Associated with this observation is the fact that what seems real is as a result of what you experience personally. If someone relates their experiences to you, say they describe a type of food you have never eaten, you may try to imagine what that food tastes like, but that imagined taste can't be said to be real taste. It only becomes real when you experience the taste of the food for yourself. Even if you believe their account of taste with conviction, that belief is not the reality.

As such, the sense of reality depends on your direct experience.

~

Secondly, if reality is a product of what is directly experienced, then it isn't necessarily limited to what you experience. It could be experienced by someone else.

Just because you've never experienced something doesn't mean that it isn't real. What you've never experienced (such as the taste of food you've never tasted) could nevertheless seem very real to someone who has experienced it. The logical conclusion is that while you depend on experience to determine what is real, reality isn't restricted to what you experience. The sense of reality may arise to someone else even if you don't personally experience it.

As such, the sense of reality depends on direct experience but not necessarily yours.

~

Having made those observations, let's consider what might be real and what might not be real. Considering our starting definition that 'reality is what is sensed or experienced', we are left with the following situation:

- What you experience is real to you but not to me. What you don't experience isn't real to you but can be real to me.

- What I experience is real to me but not to you. What I don't experience isn't real to me but can be real to you.

- I may believe your account that what you experienced is real and you may believe my account that something I experienced is real, however, that belief is not the experience of reality.

—

Having laid out this groundwork, we are presented with some interesting questions about the possible relationship between reality and experience.

Does the fact of personal experience create different classes of reality between the reality you experience and the reality you don't? Or is reality all one and the same regardless of whether you personally experience it or not?

If personal experience creates different classes of reality, what is that difference? How are these realities related to each other? Can they be ranked? Is one class more real than another?

If reality is the same whether you experience it or not, then what is the role of your experiences? Do they just filter the appearance of the reality? If so, can your experiences be said to be the reality or merely an interpretation of it? If they are just a subjective interpretation can they accurately be identified as real ... are they the reality?

And if reality isn't dictated by your personal experiences or my personal experiences, what is the nature of the reality that isn't experienced by anyone? Is it a different reality or exactly the same?

Is experience even necessary for reality? Can reality exist independently of experience?

～

You can tie yourself up in knots trying to nut this stuff out.

In my view, the task is made unnecessarily complicated because of our starting assumption that what is experienced is real.

I'd suggest that this assumption is inadequate and leads to unnecessary complication and confusion.

Rather than attempt to tie reality to experience and insist that that what is experienced *is* real, I suggest that it is better to start off with the proposition that what is experienced *seems* real.

By adopting this approach, we arrive at the situation that what you experience seems real to you, but not necessarily to those who don't experience it and what other people experience seems real to them, but not necessarily to you.

Accordingly, with regard to the illusion of water lying on the hot road, we can sensibly say that it seems real without having to insist that it is real. It follows that just as your world can appear tangible without actually being tangible ... your world can appear real without actually being the reality.

⌣

While this approach does settle many of the vexing issues raised above, it isn't a complete solution. We still haven't answered the most important question ... if our experiences and our respective worlds merely seem real, what is real? Indeed, what is reality?

This line of enquiry will be the focus of the next few chapters.

⌣

The purpose of this chapter was to consider the claim that reality is what we sense or experience.

Although that seemed like a sensible proposition, the more we tested the theory of experienced-based reality, the more complicated and less plausible it became. Reality isn't just limited to your experiences; it isn't limited to our experiences; it may not even be limited to experiences.

The possibility of a reality which isn't based on experiences is a tantalising prospect which will involve further investigation. It may even demand a fundamental reappraisal of our understanding of reality.

⌣

Despite the appearance of reality, it may be the case that your world is far more dreamlike than you have ever imagined.

Reality might not be what you have always believed ... it might be what you've never experienced and have never imagined.

As always, my intention isn't to convince you, but to encourage you to question your assumptions.

15 The illusion of Reality

Usually when we use the word 'real', we are referring to an object or event that isn't imagined, fake or make-believe. We mean that it is something which either is being experienced, has been experienced or can be experienced.

While this understanding may be sufficient for day to day communication, once we start to consider the adequacy of this definition, we find that it falls short.

For a start, not everything that you experience is necessarily real. Illusionists can cleverly and quite readily demonstrate that many perceptions you take for granted (regarding movement, distance, size, sound and colour) are tricks of the mind and are not real.

Then you have the complicating factor that your experiences represent a miniscule fraction of the total number of experiences. This suggests that there is a vast reality which you have never experienced and can never experience. It could be argued that your perspective of reality is so narrow that it may not accurately reflect the bigger-picture reality.

And if reality can exist without your personal experience of it, then it begs the question whether reality needs to be tied to experience at all.

It may be the case that the totality of all experiences doesn't capture the totality of reality. Conceivably, the totality of all experiences may represent a limitation of reality.

This is a highly interesting proposition as it disentangles us from our misguided definition that 'what is experienced is real' and raises the intriguing possibly that reality isn't tied to experiences.

~

This line of thought presents a challenge in that historically and culturally we have been conditioned to think of reality as something we can and do sense. However, if reality is not wed to experiences then it exists regardless of whether we experience it or not. In other words, reality exists in the absence of experience.

What does this tell us about reality?

If reality exists in the absence of our sensations and experiences, then this reality is not a mental image we can form in our mind. It is not an object we can observe. It is not an event we can witness. It is not a thought or a feeling. It is not anything which is a product of our consciousness. It is beyond experience. It is beyond the reaches of your world and all others.

This reality *is*, yet it is ungraspable. It defies empirical and conceptual analysis. It can't be imagined. It is beyond comprehension. And it certainly isn't tangible.

If you have only thought of reality in terms of what has been experienced, this reality (which I will refer to as 'Reality') will sorely challenge your comprehension.

~

In this chapter I want to attempt to introduce you to this concept of Reality; however, in order to do so we must settle on a more appropriate definition.

Rather than limit Reality to what can be experienced, I would like to introduce another definition ... *What is Real doesn't change.*

In this regard, Reality isn't an experience or an appearance which changes. It doesn't come and go. It isn't a passing phase. It doesn't appear as one thing one moment and something else the next. It isn't physical or tangible. It isn't even a concept.

It is permanent and unchanging.

~

What should become apparent from this definition is that as everything in your world changes, nothing in your world can be the Reality.

Even though events, objects and phenomena may seem to be real, the fact that they change demonstrates that they aren't actually real. They have the appearance of reality, but that appearance isn't the Reality.

Reality isn't any of the changing appearances of reality but instead underpins each and all of those changing appearances.

~

As this may be a challenging concept, some examples may help to clarify the issue.

If you think in terms of an on and off switch ... we could say that the Reality is the support for both on and off, but also the bridge between them.   It is that essence which is neither on nor off ... yet paradoxically is both.

Or in binary code, it is the support for 0 and 1, but also that which exists in the gap between them, which is neither 0 nor 1.

~

If you observe a cloud closely you will notice that it is constantly changing.   Each appearance is a momentary appearance in a sea of momentary appearances.

Each momentary appearance seems real; however, the Reality that I'm trying to introduce isn't any of those changing appearances.   Instead, it is the support of each appearance ... it is the gap between each appearance ... it is the bridge for all changing appearances.

It is not only the changeless essence of those appearances but the glue which binds them all together.

~

Consider this analogy ...

If you go to the beach you can watch the waves breaking on the shore. Each wave forms, surges forward and when it reaches a peak breaks into a foamy white turmoil which rushes to the shore in a million splintered pieces. Once its energy has been exhausted, the water retreats towards the sea where it is swallowed to form part of a subsequent wave.

According to conventional understanding you might think that each wave is real. However, in terms of the definition that we are currently considering, the waves are more appropriately described as momentary appearances while, borrowing from the analogy, the ocean is the underlying Reality.

While the appearance seems real, the fact that it changes demonstrates that it isn't the Reality. The Reality is unaffected by the changing appearances.

⁓

If we apply this analogy to say, a butterfly, we can see that just as the wave constantly changes, the butterfly constantly metamorphoses.

The butterfly first appears as an egg. After a period of time, the egg is transformed into a caterpillar. The caterpillar grows and then spins a cocoon where it is transformed into a chrysalis. The chrysalis is then transformed into a butterfly.

What is the Reality of the butterfly?

While any of those appearances from egg to butterfly may seem real, the Reality is none of those changing appearances. Rather, it is the foundation and continuity of all those transformations. It is the changeless essence which embodies all those changes.

~

We can also apply the concept to your own life history.

Since conception you have variously appeared as a foetus reclining in the womb, a helpless baby who makes gurgling noises, a child who plays hide and seek, an adult trying to make their way in life, and ultimately an elderly person crippled by advanced age.

Those transformations are so dramatic that you not only appear different, but atomically your body is completely different. Everything about you, the person, has changed.

What then is your Reality?

You could claim that it is this or that changing appearance. You could also claim that it is the totality of all those appearances, the bulk of which no longer exist.

Or you could consider your Reality as that unchanging essence which encompasses all of the various appearances and phases which emerge during your lifetime … including the gaps between them.

—

At this stage it is sufficient to be aware that there are alternative views of reality which may be different from what you have always assumed. Reality may not be what you experience. Instead, it may be that support which makes those experiences possible. It may be the cohesion bridging those differing experiences.

It may not be the appearance; it may be the totality which underpins all appearances.

—

If this view of Reality has any validity, then it isn't a physical phenomenon such as an ocean. It can't even be perceived. Instead, only its effects – the perception of body, mind, world – can be observed and analysed.

These effects appear real, but when they change that illusion is shattered. They are not the Reality.

The fact of change demonstrates the existence of underlying cohesion enabling all change. This Reality is the changeless factor upon which all change is predicated.

16 Reality is the incomprehensible source

The concept of Reality that was introduced in the last chapter may be difficult to grasp, especially if you've always believed that reality is what you can experience.

It may help if, in this chapter, we explore the relationship between Reality on the one hand and the appearance of reality on the other. By exploring this relationship we will be better placed to appreciate, at least conceptually, the nature of Reality.

When I say 'appearance of reality' I am referring to everything that changes, that being the entirety of what can be perceived, whether object, event, thought or feeling. All of those appearances are expressions of Reality. They are derived from Reality and are entirely dependent upon it. However, as manifestations of Reality, they can't be said to be the Reality.

Reality, on the other hand, is not a mere appearance. It is the changeless support and foundation of all changing appearances.

To borrow from the 'big bang' conceptual framework, it is that which is prior to all 'big bangs' ... and out of which all universes emerge. As the source of everything, it is the potential for everything.

Or to use my conceptual framework, it is 'prior' to all perceiving ... and out of which all perceptions emerge. As the source of all perceiving, it is the potential for all perception. Yet, it is not dependent on any appearance of reality; it isn't even affected by those appearances.

Even in the absence of all appearances, Reality *is* ... albeit absolutely unperceived and unmanifested.

~

One way to conceptualise the relationship is to think of the appearance of reality as a perception or interpretation of Reality.

Increasingly refined perceptions-interpretations result in what we would conceptually describe as subatomic particles, atoms, elements and ultimately the appearance of multidimensional worlds existing in consciousness.

As the expressions are actually just perceptions they have no substance, yet they form the intangible structure of the universe.

Whatever emerges as a result of these multiple levels of perceiving represents a filtered interpretation of Reality, the inexhaustible source potential.

~

A key feature of any resulting perception-interpretation is that it is subject to change. Atoms vibrate, stars burn, planets spin, bodies develop, consciousness appears, feelings stir, thoughts arise ... and all fades away. Everything appears, lasts its duration and disappears. All is in a state of transformation. No appearance is permanent.

Change is intrinsic to all appearances of reality. Indeed the perception of change drives those appearances. Without change there can be no appearance; there is just Reality.

These changing appearances may seem real – whether an object, a feeling, or an experience – but they are just appearances made possible by perceiving. The sense of reality associated with those appearances is not inherent in those appearances; instead it is a reflection of the underlying Reality; it is a taste of Reality.

⁓

I think that a very useful analogy to help illuminate the relationship between Reality and the appearance of reality is that of a beam of light shining through a prism and producing a rainbow effect.

The beam of light is colourless, but when refracted through the prism, it appears as colour. While the colour appears to exist independently, it is actually a product of the light. Without the light there is no colour.

The particular display of colour which emerges is determined by the qualities of the prism. Change the prism and the appearance of colour changes with it. Without the prism the particular appearance of colour doesn't emerge.

⌣

In this analogy, the light beam is like Reality, the prism is like the filter of mind-body (including its entire history), and the colour is like the world which emerges.

While your world appears to be tangible and real, it is actually a reflection of the Reality. Just as the colour has no independent existence, neither does your world. And as the colour is in essence the light, so your world is in essence the Reality.

The mind-body filter is the medium which results in the appearance of your world. That medium filters the Reality and shapes your world. As the medium changes, your world changes with it.

The Reality is the source. Colourless it is the source of all colours. Un-manifested it is the source of all manifestation. No-world it is the source of all worlds.

⌣

Just as the light beam isn't affected by any of the colours which are refracted, the Reality isn't affected by any world which emerges. The Reality doesn't change with any appearance. Even without any appearance it is unaffected. It is what it is.

The emerging worlds are, on the other hand, filtered appearances resulting from perceiving. As expressions of the Reality, they are shaped by the medium. Through different mediums, different worlds result. Any similarities or differences between worlds are explainable by the medium and its history. But without Reality, there are no worlds.

~

Every world is an expression of the Reality. A multitude of different worlds may emerge but Reality is common to all.

Those worlds are fleeting, but the Reality is permanent and perennial. Worlds change but the Reality doesn't.

~

At this very moment, your experiences are dependent on Reality. They are a reflection of Reality.

Through the medium of your mind-body (incorporating its entire history) Reality is filtered – through sub-atomic particles and ultimately consciousness and intellect – resulting in your current experiences.

This filtering produces seemingly real and tangible phenomena but all is a mental appearance arising in the conscious mind.

~

As a product of perception, this world of yours – indeed all worlds – exists as mental appearances. But what is the nature of the underlying Reality? Is it a mental phenomenon as well? Can it be perceived?

While it is useful to explain the relationship between Reality and the subsequent appearance of worlds in terms of a beam of light and the resulting refraction of colour, it would be a mistake to assume that Reality can be perceived as a concept, like a beam of light.

Reality is not even a mental phenomenon, it is before any idea you can form about it. It is the potential for all mental activity.

As such, whatever idea you form about Reality is a mental image and not what Reality is. Regardless of how you try to understand Reality, it isn't that understanding. It isn't what you think, but rather the unfathomable potential which makes thinking possible.

Reality isn't a concept and can't be comprehended conceptually. It isn't a perception and can't be perceived as such.

~

The whole purpose of this book is to lead you to the realisation of Reality.

This is crucial because the realisation of Reality is essential to self-realisation. Self-realisation is the realisation of Reality. The realisation of Reality is self-realisation. Make no mistake; your reality is Reality.

What makes this journey so challenging is that unlike everything else, Reality can't be realised as an idea or a concept or a mental image. It can't be learned. It can't be studied. It can't even be appreciated. Instead, self-realisation is more in the nature of a deep insight or epiphany. It is the realisation of what has always been known ... just not realised.

The journey is worth all effort because there is nothing better than self-realisation. It is the superlative. The realisation of your Reality is peace, happiness and truth. You simply cannot wish for more.

~

At this point it is extremely tempting to get to the heart of the matter and immediately turn our attention to the exploration of self ... and address that age old question, *What* Am I?

However, there is greater benefit in briefly postponing this exploration for several chapters to consider crucial issues such as:

- How did change appear from changelessness?

- What is the relationship between mind and matter?

- What is life?

- How did consciousness appear and what is it?

- What is the relationship between brain and mind?

- Where does world come from?

- How does love rule our lives?

- What is happiness?

- Why is there unhappiness?

Having covered this conceptual ground, we will then be better placed to directly explore the mysteries of self.

In the course of this journey, the deepest layers of being will be peeled away, revealing your incomprehensible Reality beyond being.

The book will guide you every step of the way … but the journey has to be your own.

⁓

Let's delve further into the Reality underpinning all appearances of reality.

17 Reality as nothing

Let's recap our understanding of Reality so far.

We defined Reality as changeless, noting that it is the changeless background bridging all change. However, more than mere background, we noted that it is the ultimate source of all changing appearances. Everything is an expression of Reality. Those expressions result from multiple levels of perceiving and exist as perception. They might seem real but they are just filtered interpretations of the source Reality. They are products of the Reality, but aren't the Reality.

Reality isn't a perceivable phenomenon and can't be conceived as a concept. Whatever phenomena you perceive and whatever concept you form, the Reality is not that.

To be comprehended, Reality must be realised intuitively without conceptual thought. You must realise your Reality for yourself without intellectual frameworks, without ideas and without knowledge.

~

As your Reality can't be taught to you, self-realisation may seem like a hopeless task … but it isn't.

While you can't learn what you are, by focusing on mistaken assumptions which prevent you from realising what you are, the obstacles to self-realisation can be powerfully shaken.

In the absence of all misunderstanding, your Reality is self-evident. It is clear. It is obvious. It is what you have always known ... just forgotten.

~

Let's continue our exploration by considering Reality from another perspective.

To start with think about 'everything'. I don't mean just a lot of stuff; think about the entirety of 'everything' ... from the very small to the very big, from mind to matter, from past to future, from right here to way over there.

Now, once you have formed that image, I would like you to try and imagine the complete absence of everything.

I guess that if you tried to describe the image you formed in your mind, you would describe it as 'nothing'. This is a logical response. However, while the word 'nothing' seems to be a very useful fit, what does it actually mean? What is 'nothing'?

In that nothing there is no universe, no suns or planets, and no atoms or elements. There is no perception or understanding, no perceived or perceiver or even perceiving, no thoughts or feelings, no consciousness, no past or future, no here or there, no now. There isn't even your idea of 'nothing' because, after all, that is ... something. There is just NOTHING.

This 'nothing' is another way of describing the Reality which underpins all changing appearances.

~

Even though we use the word 'nothing' and may think that we understand it, actually the true significance of that word is beyond comprehension. It defies all intellectual handling.

'Nothing' is beyond categorisation. Concepts of space and time, abstract and concrete, energy and non-energy, existence and non-existence don't approach it.

It can't be perceived or imagined, let alone described or analysed. It can't be proven or disproven, yet it is undeniable.

Why undeniable? Because the existence of anything presupposes its non-existence. The appearance of anything presupposes its non-appearance. The presence of anything presupposes its absence.

~

There is, however, another aspect of 'nothing' which I would like to share with you.

While you may think of 'nothing' as the absence of everything, which it is, I would also encourage you to think of that 'nothing' as the source of 'everything'.

Inasmuch as Reality is the changeless source of all change, so 'nothing' is the source of 'everything'. That 'nothing' is the essence from which 'everything' emerged. 'Everything' is an expression of 'nothing'. The filtering of 'nothing' results in the appearance of 'everything'.

～

Of course, this approach demands a reassessment of what we mean by 'nothing'. As the source of 'everything', this 'nothing' is the infinite and inexhaustible potential for everything that ever will be ... but also never will be.

It is the non-dimensional source of all dimensions: spacelessness expressed in space, timelessness expressed in time. It is the unmanifest source of all manifestation and non-manifestation.

That 'nothing' is the primordial original state. It is the essence of everything and is everything in essence.

Everything is its expression. Everything is its reflection.

～

When considering the 'nothing', words cannot suffice.

It is the immutable support of everything. It is the unbroken continuity behind all change. It is the order in chaos; the actual in the conceptual; the permanent in the temporary; the reality in the appearance. It is the root of here and now: the soul of all.

It pervades all but nothing is it. It is in all but beyond all. It contains all but nothing contains it. It is altogether transcendent. It is whole and complete, indivisible and changeless, pure and perfect, limitless and unconstrainable. It is the absence of absence, the fullness of fullness.

~

Consider 'nothing' as just a word to help explain a different aspect of Reality. Many other words have been used ... Absolute, Void, Truth, Self.

All those words refer to the same essence. However, none even begin to capture it.

That essence can't be realised conceptually ... but it can be realised. Once everything else is perceived in its correct perspective, Reality is clear and obvious.

~

If you ask me "*what* is it?" ... words aren't sufficient.

It is the ultimate Reality.

I am it. You are it too.

You have to realise it for yourself.

18 The absence of concepts

When we discuss the Reality we are, of course, considering it conceptually. The Reality, however, is not a conceptual phenomenon and can't be understood conceptually.

As such, it is not surprising that it is difficult to arrive at a half suitable analogy that might give some insight, albeit conceptual, into the Reality, but here goes ...

~

In this exercise, try and think of yourself as being blue.

Now, the only reason you know that you are blue is because you are able to compare and differentiate yourself from other colours such as red, green or yellow. If you couldn't compare your colour against any other colours, you would have no point of reference to know that other colours exist and your colour is blue.

The next step in the exercise is to then imagine that everything around you is also this exact shading of blue. There are no shadows or tones to give texture, contrast or context.

In this blue world everything appears exactly the same and you are unable to differentiate anything around you.

You can't even distinguish your blue self from your blue environment. All is indistinguishably blue.

When all is blue there is no appearance of difference, change or otherness. All is one. And blueness is all.

However, because blueness is all ... you don't know that you are blue; you don't even know that you are. There is no you.

~

This imagery can help to conceptualise the Reality.

Instead of being a colour, picture the Reality as the potential for everything. That potential is absolutely full and complete. It is everything (and more) in its absolutely unrealised form.

However, just as blue can't be recognised in a world of blue, unrealised potential can't be recognised in a 'world' of unrealised potential. While the unrealised potential is a fact, because all is unrealised potential there is no recognition of that fact.

As such, the Reality *is* but has no concept that it is ... and certainly has no concept about what it is. It is absolutely devoid of concepts. It is non-conceptual.

~

Just as blueness can only be recognised by reference to the presence of other colours, so the unrealised potential of the Reality can only be recognised when there is a point of differentiation, such as the appearance of otherness or change ... or, in other words, when that unrealised potential is realised.

However, whereas the recognition of blueness gives rise to the concept of blue ... the recognition of the Reality gives rise to an infinite number of unique conceptual interpretations of the Reality.

Those conceptual interpretations form the length and breadth of the conceptual universe, of which your world is an integral yet insignificant part.

~

The recognition of Reality is always a conceptual interpretation made possible by the appearance of a point of contradistinction.

Without that differentiation all is indistinguishable and incomprehensible Reality. There is nothing to be recognised and nothing to do the recognising.

~

As I indicated at the start of the chapter, it is impossible to conceptually understand the Reality.

Whatever concept you entertain is an interpretation made possible because of a point of differentiation.

In contrast, Reality is the complete absence of all concepts, ideas and points of reference.

There is little point trying to intellectualise the Reality ... the more you try to understand, the more it will escape you.

At this stage, it is better to appreciate the fact of the Reality, without trying to understand it.

19 Awareness of Awareness

The Reality is impossible to conceptualise and yet out of this non-conceptual Reality a multitude of conceptual worlds appear which differ widely, variously and endlessly.

One of the great mysteries is how this non-conceptual Reality came to be expressed conceptually; or in other words, how 'nothing' came to be expressed as 'everything'.

Undoubtedly, this is one of the most profoundly challenging questions we can pose. It is especially problematic because so much of the question is unanswerable.

How can we sensibly respond to the question 'how can something appear out of nothing?' when we can't comprehend 'nothing' and most probably can't comprehend the 'something' which appears?

I would go so far as to say that there can't be a conceptually correct response. Nevertheless, bearing these extreme restrictions at the forefront of mind, for the sake of completeness I will attempt to provide a conceptual answer which encapsulates my understanding as best as I can.

As you might appreciate, this will, of necessity, involve theoretical discussion; however, I'll do my best to keep it at a minimum. Is it necessary to agree with my attempted answer? Absolutely not!

~

To set the scene, if you look at a mirror you can easily see a reflection of yourself. If you look at a bank of 12 mirrors you can see 12 reflections. And if you position those 12 mirrors around you, it is possible to see reflections of reflections, thereby greatly increasing the number of reflections of yourself.

Similarly, if you could look at an infinite number of mirrors and position them so that they reflect reflections, there would be an infinite number of reflections. And if every one of those mirrors was uniquely distorted there would be an infinite number of uniquely different reflections of you.

Yet, regardless of the number and diversity of reflections, there would be just one you.

This provides an insight into the relationship between the Reality and the appearances which make up the universe.

~

There is one Reality which is expressed as an infinite number of appearances ... as an infinite number of interpretations ... as an infinite number of perceptions.

These expressions are similar to the infinite number of reflections which appear in an infinite number of mirrors.

They can range from the miniscule to the enormous, from the ancient to the new, from the simple to the complex, from the pre-conscious to the conscious, from the non-organic to the organic, from the perception of mind to the appearance of matter, from the accurate to the mistaken.

The expressions are infinitely varied, but the Reality is one. The Reality is the essence of all expressions and all expressions are its reflection.

Having set the scene, let's turn our attention to the point of this chapter ... how do we get from Reality to an infinite number of expressions? How can anything arise out of nothing? How do we get from nothing to something? How can nothing be expressed infinitely? How can everything be a reflection of nothing?

If I were to try and formulate an answer to these questions, I would suggest that while there are many ways to consider Reality – you can think of it as changeless, the source, 'nothing', non-conceptual, potential – in the light of our current discussion it is most helpful if we can think of Reality in terms of awareness.

Consider Reality as naturally and inherently aware. It is aware without being aware of anything. Without points of differentiation there is nothing to be aware of and nothing to be aware. There is just pure Awareness.

However, the very fact of this inherent awareness produces an interesting phenomenon. While there isn't anything to be aware of ... there remains the possibility of Awareness becoming aware of its Awareness.

This 'self' awareness produces an intriguing result. While Reality is indivisibly one, when Awareness is aware of its Awareness, two perspectives are created. First, there is the perspective of the Awareness which is observed. We can call that the observed Awareness or object Awareness.

Second, there is the perspective of the Awareness which observes. We can call that the observer Awareness or subject Awareness.

As such, while the Awareness of Reality is indivisible and devoid of all concepts, the fact of Awareness creates the conceptual appearance of two awarenesses ... awareness as subject and awareness as object.

In effect, by just being aware, the concept of otherness, and therefore a point of differentiation, is created. The result is that Awareness appears conceptually as two. This is the conceptual duality of subject and object.

That conceptual appearance is, of course, an entirely conceptual construct. It results from perceiving and exists as a perception. In actuality though there is no otherness, there is just Reality. There aren't two types of awareness, there is just Awareness.

⁓

The conceptualisation of Awareness into subject awareness and object awareness is the very first hint of conceptuality. It represents the dawn of perceiving and the 'birth' of the conceptual universe ... of all conceptual universes.

Crucially, this birth isn't represented by the emergence of an ancient and exotic sub-atomic particle but, rather, the non-tangible phenomenon of perceiving. That perceiving, which arises as an expression of Awareness, results in the perception of subject and object. Each perception is a reflection of Reality. An infinite number of perceptions are the reflection of Reality.

The appearance of subject and object is not indicative of tangible phenomena, but conceptual appearances. They appear but they aren't tangible; they may appear real but they aren't the Reality.

⁓

If this analysis is in anyway correct we could expect that everything which arises from this process would bear the distinctive marker of these fundamental ingredients.

First, everything (from the simplest to the most complex appearance) should be built upon non-conceptual, pure

Awareness. In other words, the deepest essence of anything should be Reality.

Second, at a fundamental conceptual level, whatever emerges should require a point of differentiation in order to appear. As such, it should take the perspective of either subject or object.

Third, associated with this conceptual separation into 'subject' and 'object', if one arises so must the other. There cannot be a subject without an object or an object without a subject.

Fourth, as a product of perceiving, whatever is perceived should have the substance of perception. It should be non-tangible.

⁓

I would suggest that this is exactly the situation we are confronted with in the universe.

First, every appearance, irrespective of how complex or insignificant, is built upon Reality. That Reality is the continuity – the changeless support – which bridges all changing appearances.

Second, whatever appears takes the perspective of either subject or object; it is either something or not something else. A point of differentiation is always present.

Third, whatever emerges always appears with its opposing but intrinsic counterpart. Any subject always has an object and any object always has a subject. They appear together because they define each other.

Fourth, while any world may appear remarkably diverse and complex it is a product of perceiving. The resulting perception takes shape as the appearance of subject or object. There is no tangible reality to these appearances; they are entirely conceptual.

Despite appearances, all is in essence Awareness: all is indivisibly one and the same.

~

Given the subject matter of this chapter and the next few, theoretical discussion is perhaps unavoidable. However, this discussion is necessary for completeness and can afford a more comprehensive overview.

That said, self-realisation doesn't require this level of conceptual understanding. It isn't necessary that you understand every theoretical point and certainly isn't necessary that you agree.

To the contrary, the concepts that are being discussed cannot lead you to realisation. At best, they can remove mistaken assumptions which may prevent realisation. Once you realise what you are, all is clear and these concepts aren't necessary.

~

In the meantime, practice this exercise to foster intuitive understanding.

When you look in the mirror and see your reflection, there appears to be four factors ... your body, your mind, the mirror and the reflection.

Realise the reflection as a product of your body, mind and mirror, and the four factors are reduced to three.

Acknowledge your body and the mirror as aspects of the one conceptual image appearing in mind and the three are reduced to one.

Then recognise your mind, which encompasses the reflection, the mirror and your body as an expression of Reality ... and you will be close to realising Reality as the infinite potential beyond.

⁓

Everything is the expression of Reality.

20 'I' and 'not-I'

In the beginning was the concept 'I'. It surveyed its world and called it 'other-than-I'. And 'I' was happy with its concept.

On the second day 'I' started to explore its world and came across a representative of 'other-than-I'.

'I' said, "It is good to meet you. Allow me to introduce myself. I am 'I' and you must be 'other-than-I'". The representative looking rather surprised responded, "It is good to meet you too, however, you are mistaken ... it is you who is 'other-than-I' ... I am 'I'".

'I' looked suspiciously at the representative and said, "Oh no that cannot be! I am the first concept. I am 'I'". The representative shaking his head said, "I'm sorry but you are wrong, I am the first concept and you are my secondary concept. You are 'other-than-I' ... I am 'I'".

They then looked at each other blankly and said, "How can this be? How can we both be 'I'? One of us must be mistaken ... but which one?"

By the third day, the two concepts worked out a solution to their dilemma. They decided to find a third concept to tell them which of them was 'I' and which one was 'other-than-I'.

The third concept was duly happened upon and informed of the impasse which had arisen. They then said, "So please resolve this conflict ... which one of us is 'I' and which one is 'other-than-I'?" Both concepts expecting vindication waited for the response.

The new concept looked thoughtful and after nodding knowingly said, "You've certainly come to the right concept to resolve your dilemma. Neither of you is 'I' ... you are both 'other-than-I'".

Visibly shocked by this answer they asked perplexedly, "But how can you say that?"

The new concept looked smug and said, "Because I am 'I' and you both are clearly 'other-than-I'".

⁓

Once the pure awareness of Reality is expressed conceptually, it takes shape as the duality 'I' and 'not-I' ... which is just another way of saying that it takes shape as the dichotomy of subject and object ... 'I' is the subject ... 'not-I' is the object.

In this chapter we will consider the relationship between these seemingly opposing appearances. Given the nature of the subject matter, the focus will be on theory.

The first point to note is that every perception which arises takes the stance of concept 'I' and perceives all else as concept 'not-I'.

The second point to note is that the situation is more complicated because what is perceived as 'not-I', perceives itself as concept 'I' ... and from that perspective interprets all else as 'not-I'.

So while all is perceived from the perspective of 'I' ... to all else it appears as 'not-I'.

Whether something is 'I' or 'not-I' is just a matter of perspective. In any appearance of 'not-I' is 'I' and in any sense of 'I' is 'not-I'. As subject ... all is 'I'. As object ... all is 'not-I'.

Despite appearances to the contrary, when viewed subjectively any interaction is actually between concept 'I' and concept 'I', or when viewed objectively between concept 'not-I' and concept 'not-I'.

It is a tricky concept to grasp, but not insurmountable.

~

'I' isn't necessarily an intellectualised, emotionalised or even conscious understanding, rather, it is the sense 'I' in rawest form. It is the primitive, unarticulated awareness 'I'. It isn't a physical phenomenon; it is more in the nature of a perspective. It is not only evidenced in humans and other life forms, but also trees and even rocks, atoms and electrons. It is present in the very first appearance. It is the perspective 'I' that gives the sense of identity, again not in a thinking or feeling sense, but in the sense which allows an electron to behave like an electron, an atom to behave like an atom, a rock to behave like a rock or a human like a human.

That fundamental perspective of 'I' is the building block of any universe. Without it there cannot be a conceptual universe.

~

The concept 'I' may be the primary concept – the building block of everything – but it can't be separated from concept 'not-I'.

'Not-I' isn't an intellectual or emotional understanding. It is the perspective 'not-I' in its rawest form. It is the primitive, unarticulated awareness 'not-I'. It is a perception, not a physical phenomenon. It is the crudest concept of otherness or separation that can exist. It is the sense and appearance of difference. It not only keeps atom separate from atom, but human separate from human.

The concept 'not-I' is crucial to the development of the universe. Without the appearance of 'not-I' there is no universe ... and not even the concept 'I'.

~

While we may think of 'I' as the first concept it actually arises in tandem as an intrinsic expression of 'not-I'.

The perspective of 'I' is always a reflection of its perception of 'not-I'. 'Not-I' defines the 'I' just as much as 'I' defines the 'not-I'. As two aspects of the one, they are mirrors of each other.

Accordingly, 'I' and 'not-I' shape each other. As the concept 'I' changes, so does the concept 'not-I'. And, as the concept 'not-I' changes, so does the concept 'I'.

However, as 'I' and 'not-I' are entirely conceptual appearances, the potential number of combinations and variations are infinitely varied. The only limitation of 'I' is concept 'not-I' and the only limitation of 'not-I' is the concept 'I'.

~

While 'I' and 'not-I' may appear different they are reflections of each other. As mirror images, they don't just possess a symbiotic relationship, they are two aspect of the one. They are one and the same.

It is an understatement to say that 'I' and 'not-I' are infinitely interconnected. They are one and the same. There is absolutely no division or separation. What appears to be 'not-I' is actually 'I' and what appears to be 'I' is actually 'not-I'.

As the expression of the one Reality 'I' and 'not-I' are one. Any appearance of difference is conceptual only ... an illusion. In actuality there is no difference.

Everything that ever appears is one and the same.

~

It's not necessary that you agree with or even understand every fine point that is raised in this chapter, but hopefully you will find some interest in the perspective.

Of course, the chapter doesn't have to remain a purely theoretical exercise. You can apply these principles to your own life.

While the person you think you are may seem to be 'I', to everything else it appears to be 'not-I'. Which perspective, then, is correct? Are you 'I' or are you 'not-I'?

If you think that you are just 'I', examine that belief closely and you will discover that your concept is defined by your unarticulated concept 'not-I'.

Indeed, your concept 'I' is so entirely dependent on concept 'not-I' as to be inseparable. What you think you are ('I') cannot exist in the absence of what you think you aren't ('not-I').

What then are you? 'I', 'not-I', both or neither?

~

Believing that 'I' and 'not-I' are separate realities is an insurmountable obstacle to the apperception of Reality. Instead, understand all permutations of 'I' and 'not-I' as seemingly different aspects of the one mental image … mere conceptual appearances of the one Awareness.

While that Awareness gives birth to all expressions of 'I' and 'not-I', it isn't any of those conceptual divisions. Instead it is whole and complete. It is the non-conceptual and unfathomable Reality.

That Reality is your Reality.

21 Mind and Matter

Having introduced my attempt at explaining the birth of the conceptual universe, we will now consider the appearance of mind and matter.

So far we've noted that Reality is the subtle but untraceable source of everything which appears. It is the potential for all manifestation.

This potential is realised when Reality is expressed as the conceptual duality of subject 'I' and object 'not-I'. This conceptualisation represents the birth of the conceptual universe.

Everything that subsequently emerges is a permutation of that duality. Everything that appears is infused with the awareness of Reality and has the sense of being the subject 'I' but the appearance of being an object 'not-I'.

Crucially, in this paradigm all is perceived from the perspective of 'I' ... 'I' perceives 'not-I'. As such 'not-I' is a perception of 'I'; however, without the perception of 'not-I' there is no 'I'.

~

This dichotomy represents the appearance of mind and matter. Mind is the perception 'I'. Matter is the perception 'not-I'. Mind perceives matter. Matter is a perception of mind.

Without wanting to complicate this already complex issue, we could also observe that mind is memory and matter is what is remembered. In this regard, matter represents the concept 'space' and mind represents the concept 'time' ... the memory of changing 'space'.

Crucially though, neither mind nor matter remain static. Matter is shaped by the mind which perceives. Mind is shaped by the matter which is perceived.

As mind and matter are interpreted and reinterpreted, perception is built upon perception, and increasingly complex concepts of both emerge. This interplay of the concepts of mind and matter represent the universe in various stages of refinement.

～

From the perspective of the modern western mind, we interpret these various stages of conceptual refinement as:

- The expression of the 'big bang' from the Reality.

- The emergence of sub-atomic particles, resulting in the appearance of hydrogen and helium atoms.

- The reaction between these atoms, resulting in clouds of hydrogen and the release of radiation and light.

- The condensation of these clouds, resulting in the formation of stars.

- The fusion within stars generating starlight and the formation of heavier elements.

- The supernova of massive stars blasting their matter and energy into space.

- The coalescence of that debris to form stars and planets revolving around those suns.

- The complex interactions of elements, resulting in the appearance of amino acids, proteins, ribonucleic acid (RNA) and deoxyribonucleic acid (DNA).

- The emergence of cellular structures, ultimately resulting in a multitude of life forms ranging from bacteria to plants and insect to animals.

~

When we consider these processes it is tempting to think of evolution solely in terms of matter ... sub-atomic particles leading to atoms leading to stars. However, this is only part of the equation. The other vital ingredient is mind.

Even if you are aware of the role of mind, it would be a mistake to assume that mind is a static phenomenon, merely witnessing the evolution of matter.

Instead, the process incorporates the evolution of both mind and matter. When matter evolves so does mind. Actually, it is the evolution of mind which enables the perception, and hence creation, of the more complex constructs of matter. Those more complex constructs of matter are perceptions of mind and are indicative of the stage of development of mind.

While we cannot directly observe the evolution of the non-conscious aspects of mind, we can indirectly witness (albeit through the filter of consciousness) that evolution through its changing perceptions, which are expressed as evolving matter.

The evolution of matter reflects the evolution of mind. In fact, the evolution of matter is the evolution of mind.

⁓

We can't be sure of the exact dynamics of the mind-matter compact which results in the conceptual appearance of a sub-atomic particle or an atom, element or cell. At this stage we can only say that it was a natural development resulting from the prevailing environment.

Those prevailing conditions determine the appearance or non-appearance of a sub-atomic particle, the emergence of this or that atom, the materialisation of a sun here as opposed to there, the shape and structure of this galaxy as opposed to that.

Environmental conditions also determine the chemical composition of planets and their placement in a solar system. And those conditions in turn determine whether a planet is capable of sustaining living organisms or not.

~

Not only is any appearance of mind or matter the direct expression of the prevailing environment, but it does not exist separately to that environment.

As such, any new perception/appearance which arises, in turn, forms part of the prevailing environment out of which subsequent perceptions/appearances emerge.

It is also very interesting to note that, while more complex permutations of mind and matter appear, the underlying Reality remains unchanged.

What this tells us is that while the process of perceiving results in more complex permutations of mind and matter, it does not create that complexity. Instead, it merely realises the complexity latently inherent in the Reality.

As such, everything that emerges is an expression of its environment ... and that environment is an expression of Reality.

The realisation of any complexity is the realisation of the inexhaustible potential inherent in Reality.

~

While we are discussing the topic, allow me to make a few more observations about the nature of a universe comprised of mind-matter.

Firstly, when we talk about the prevailing environment producing any given appearance, we are actually saying that it is an expression of that environment. However, more than just an expression, any appearance is, in fact, a unique encapsulation of that environment.

And inasmuch as the reaches of any environment are universal in nature, any appearance is both expression and encapsulation of everything else.

This is an intriguing point, so allow me to use an example – a rock – to explain. Its formation is not only due to the geological forces that went into its creation, but also the cosmological forces that created the earth, the atomic forces that created elements and the quantum forces that created sub-atomic particles. That entire history is reflected in the rock. The rock is the encapsulation of that entire history.

The rock is such an encapsulation of that history that if it were possible to annihilate just a grain of the rock, the rest of the conceptual universe would be annihilated with it.

Why? Because, the annihilation of the grain would by implication involve the annihilation of the entire history which went into its formation. As such, this would not only annihilate the grain but also the universe which relies on the self-same building blocks.

~

Secondly, another interesting aspect of this conceptual universe is the cause and effect relationship.

As we've just noted, anything which appears is the expression of everything else. In other words, everything else is the cause of anything.

However, the very existence of anything has a subsequent effect (even if negligible) on anything else that appears, in which case the effect becomes the cause.

It may be a theoretical point, but we are left with the fascinating situation that everything is the cause of everything ... and everything is the effect of everything. Everything is both cause and effect.

~

Thirdly, I would strongly suggest that these types of intriguing properties are only possible because we are dealing with constantly changing conceptual appearances ... and most definitely not tangible realities. In this conceptual universe, everything is intrinsically related to everything. Nothing is independent of anything else. Any appearance is a product of the total environment and is the encapsulation of that total environment.

In everything is anything and in anything is everything. The difference is only in appearance.

That appearance arises because of the dichotomy of Awareness into conceptual mind and matter. Without that dichotomy all is just Reality.

~

This has been another theoretical chapter. Hopefully, you will appreciate the subject matter; but if not, rest assured that we will be turning our attention to a direct exploration of self, where our attention will be firmly taken with practical matters.

However, before doing so we will continue our exploration and over the next few chapters consider the nature of life and trace the emergence of consciousness, the appearance of mental images, the development of the person, the experience of love and happiness, and the conditioning which encourages people to pursue the good life.

22 Life is all

Of all the unanswered questions that confront man, one of the most intriguing concerns the origins of life. When and how did life emerge?

This issue is so crucial that any consideration of the evolution of Reality into the world you are familiar with must address the emergence of life. However first, we must ask ourselves what we mean by the word "life". What is life? Is it an animal that can think and communicate? A plant that can breathe and metabolise? A bacterium that can respond and adapt? A virus that can grow and reproduce?

Certainly, these are all common characteristics of life forms, but what actually is life? What is the life in all these life-forms?

In this chapter I will share my perspective on this most challenging subject.

⁓

To approach this question it is necessary to question ingrained and possibly mistaken assumptions about life.

Indeed, just by asking 'what is life?' we may be setting up a false dichotomy of systems into non-living and living. It may be that just asking this question betrays a false assumption about the nature of life.

—

So let's start by considering when we think life started.

Did it start with the appearance of the first living organism or did life actually pre-exist the appearance of that first organism?

If you are like most people, you will probably think that life commenced with the emergence of the first organism and that before this appearance there was just a lifeless environment of minerals, metals and other compounds.

This view represents generally accepted wisdom; however, I want to suggest an alternative view. Life pre-existed the first organism.

The environment itself was life.

—

While that environment may appear – in the absence of more familiar life forms – to have been lifeless, it actually gave birth to the first organism.

As such, it is not only the source of the organism, but also the source of life in that organism. And as the source of life it is, in essence, life.

Arguably, the first living organism (which is, after all, a chemical system with the ability to grow and self-sustain by gathering energy from the surroundings) didn't miraculously appear out of what was a lifeless environment. Instead, that environment was life in embryonic form. And from out of that environment more complex expressions of life – such as living organisms – emerged.

In this sense, the appearance of life in the organism is an expression of the life which was pre-existing in the environment.

～

This view doesn't restrict its understanding of life to a few behavioural characteristics which more obviously demonstrate the existence of life. Nor does it attempt to separate life forms from the environment from which they emerge.

Instead, it adopts a holistic approach. Life is viewed as one continuous and unbroken process of development, while most obviously commencing with the birth of the conceptual universe … actually having its source in the Reality. The entire universe itself is seen as life.

In this regard, life first manifested when Awareness was perceived in duality and was subsequently expressed as mind and matter, subatomic and atomic particles, inorganic and organic compounds, living organisms and more complex life forms.

Life is the expression of Reality. Everything is life in action.

⌣

This doesn't mean that there is nothing to be gained from exploring the complex geological and chemical processes which resulted in the first appearance of biological phenomena (i.e. living organisms). However, it may be counter-productive to assume that life is restricted to those subsequent biological processes. Instead, greater insights may be afforded if those formative geological and chemical processes are also seen as expressions of life.

I would suggest that any attempt to isolate, and thereby limit, life can only result in misunderstanding.

⌣

When life is perceived in this holistic sense it becomes clear that life can't be categorised or pigeon-holed. It is in everything and everything is it.

Particular expressions of life may be limited, but life itself is unlimited and can't be exhausted.

Life doesn't depend on its expressions. All expressions depend on life.

While those expressions may appear and disappear, life is unaffected. Indeed, lives come and go, but life is impervious. Atoms may be split and galaxies may be devoured, but life remains whole and complete. It is one and remains one.

Life is the cause. Life is the effect. It is both creation and destruction. Even death is an expression of life.

—

I don't think that this chapter raises any deeply challenging concepts; however, let me finish by sharing an analogy.

Life is like a block of gold which is moulded and remoulded into a variety of ornaments. The shape of the ornaments may change, but the gold is the same. Regardless of how the gold is moulded, it remains gold.

Even though countless ornaments appear and disappear, none of that gold is lost. And no matter how much the gold is reworked, its ability to be remoulded is never diminished.

The appearance of one ornament may entail the disappearance of another, but the gold itself is immutable.

—

While the image of melting and moulding gold into ornaments may suggest deliberate action, in the case of life, all functioning results from entirely automatic processes of mere random, yet orderly, attraction and repulsion.

All is determined by prevailing environmental conditions.

In this equation nothing is imposed. Life functions without intention or effort. There is no goal or purpose; all is just a natural and spontaneous expression of life interacting with life.

The appearance of order among all expressions of life is the natural expression of life. It is the reflection of the perfection of Reality.

~

It's not necessary to agree with the perspective offered in this chapter. It would, however, seem that any understanding of life is unnecessarily complicated if expression is separated from source, and artificially divided into concepts of life and non-life.

Instead, I would suggest that life is beyond such classifications. Life is not this or that. It is one and encompasses everything. It may appear as many but is, in fact, all. Nothing is separate from life because life is all there is.

23 The light of consciousness

Undoubtedly one of the most crucial events in the long history of everything – at least from our perspective – is the emergence of consciousness.

Prior to the advent of consciousness there was Reality. Initially, it was expressed as the concepts of 'I' and 'not-I', which subsequently evolved into more complex concepts which we describe as sub-atomic particles, atoms, elements, molecular compounds and more latterly multicellular organisms.

These expressions were aware, but not consciously aware. Despite great advances, self-awareness was not a conscious phenomenon. There was no sense of existence, no sensations, and no mental images.

Quite opportunely, the expressions of Reality did not cease with the appearance of non-conscious multicellular life, but continued, resulting in perhaps its crowning achievement ... consciousness.

~

Consciousness is not only a significant phenomenon in the history of the universe, it's a significant phenomenon in your life.

By virtue of consciousness you are able to sense and experience, be self-aware and know that you are alive. It is only because of consciousness that you are able to experience your world and consider its intricacies and relationship to you. Indeed, without consciousness your world doesn't exist.

In this chapter we will consider the emergence of consciousness. How did it arise and why do you experience consciousness? Why is it that you can be conscious of, say, a rock, but it isn't conscious of you?

Before addressing these issues, there are a couple of definitional matters which I would like to clarify upfront.

- When I use the word 'awareness', I am referring to that primordial ability to perceive. It is that core ability to differentiate 'I' from 'not-I'. It is the prerequisite for all non-conscious perception.

- In contrast, when I use the word 'consciousness', I am referring to an advanced expression of 'awareness'. It may be described as the sense of being, the knowledge 'I exist', the perception 'I am'. It is the *sensation* of existence. It is the pre-requisite for subsequent conscious perception.

While we are discussing definitional issues, I'll take the opportunity to remind you that it should be taken as given that when I use words such as "atom", "matter", "chemical", "rock", "body", "world", "universe" or even "awareness" or "consciousness" I am referring to conceptual appearances arising in the conscious mind. Ultimately, I am not suggesting that they exist as anything other than products of perceiving.

～

Perhaps the simplest way to consider the emergence of consciousness is to consider the history of your body.

If you believe that your body has only existed since birth, this might seem like a strange approach. However, when you consider that your body was not 'new' at birth but billions of years old, the approach is not without merit.

How can your body have been billions of years old?

Well, while it might have appeared new at birth, the atoms which give your body structure were formed in the crucibles of space, the elements which sustain your body were forged in the heart of ancient stars, and the genetic material which shapes your body grew out of the dust of the Earth. Already at the instant of birth your body was the encapsulation of a multi-billion year history that went into its making.

For the vast majority of that history your body was not conscious and had no way of entertaining these ideas that you are currently reading and contemplating. Sure, there was awareness expressed as (what we would call) atoms, elements and genetic material, but not consciousness.

In terms of that history, consciousness is only a very recent phenomenon. It is not until living organisms had not only emerged but evolved that consciousness appeared.

Only when the matter of your body had organised into the structure of a sufficiently complex organism could consciousness emerge.

When expressed that consciousness was experienced as a sensation, but not just any sensation. It was the very first sensation, the sensation of existence.

While just a sensation, it radicalised perceiving and the resulting perceptions.

~

What observations about the appearance of consciousness can we make?

We can certainly note that consciousness is a product of the prevailing conditions existing in the environment. It is neither a separate phenomenon nor externally imposed. It is a natural expression of awareness.

However, consciousness is not a product of just any environmental conditions. If our experience on Earth is any guide, it requires a highly specialised set of conditions, the chief requirement being an extreme degree of complexity. This level of complexity is indicated by the presence of advanced living organisms.

As such, while awareness is present in atoms, elements and compounds; consciousness only arises in sufficiently complex organisms. Such complexity represents the right environmental conditions for mind to mature into consciousness ... for 'I' to be expressed as 'I am'.

~

If those conditions don't emerge then neither does consciousness. If the required complexity of matter does not arise, the exact same commonplace ingredients which currently comprise your body (substantially oxygen, carbon, hydrogen, nitrogen, calcium and phosphorus) could readily exist as inorganic chemicals and compounds ... aware but bereft of consciousness.

Without the required complexity, consciousness is not expressed. It remains as unrealised potential in the environment. It persists as a non-conscious state of awareness ... a less developed state of mind. It is latent in less complex appearances of matter.

One configuration will obscure consciousness, but another configuration of exactly the same matter will reveal it. What makes all the difference is the progression of mind.

~

While some people may view the appearance of consciousness as a miraculous expression of matter, I would suggest that the mind-matter duality is the crucial ingredient.

What we observe as the increasing complexity of evolving matter actually represents the increasing ability of mind to perceive. It is this perceptual ability of the mind which creates more complex and nuanced permutations of matter.

The evolution of matter into a complex living organism is due to the deepening perceptual abilities of the mind, ultimately resulting in the appearance of consciousness. This appearance is indicative that the mind has evolved sufficiently to express awareness as consciousness.

If we just focus on the appearance of matter it is easy to overlook the fact of the evolving mind.

~

Interestingly, it is functioning at the non-conscious levels of mind which result in the appearance of consciousness. As such, consciousness is not only a product of non-conscious processes, but requires the continuation of those processes in order to manifest.

If those non-conscious processes (which drive the required complexity) are not maintained, the consciousness dissolves and reverts to its prior non-conscious state.

Another way of expressing this point is to say that consciousness not only depends on the appearance of a sufficiently complex living organism, but will only continue with the support of that organism. Without such support the appearance of consciousness cannot be maintained.

In other words, if the mind-body cannot sustain the necessary complexity – as in the case of severe injury or death – consciousness cannot be supported and will revert to its non-conscious but aware state in the non-conscious ocean of the mind.

Consciousness doesn't exist independently of the mind-body which fuels its appearance.

~

In my view, a living body is the vehicle of consciousness. If no such body emerges there is no consciousness.

If a living body materialises consciousness appears. However, it only lasts the life of the body. It doesn't survive its 'death'.

In the absence of a living body there is awareness but no conscious awareness; life but no conscious life; perception but no conscious perception.

~

As an aside, while it can be said that a living body gives rise to consciousness, it is only because of consciousness that the body can be perceived consciously.

As such, while body reveals consciousness ... consciousness reveals body.

This situation directly parallels the mind-matter relationship where mind is revealed through matter and matter is revealed through mind.

＿

To summarise, consciousness is an expression of awareness ... a reflection of Reality.

It is a naturally occurring phenomenon resulting from universal processes.

Consciousness is only expressed with the perception of significant complexity. That complexity is characterised by an advanced life form.

In the absence of a living body there is no consciousness. And in the absence of consciousness there is no world.

Consciousness is the light which transforms everything.

24 The image of world

The next step to consider is that of the appearance of the conscious mind and, indeed, the world as you know it.

We've made the point that consciousness emerges as a result of increasingly complex perceptions at the level of the non-conscious mind. However, this mental evolution didn't stop with the appearance of consciousness. It continued, resulting in further refinements of the mind's ability to perceive and the associated appearance of more complex permutations of matter.

These developments resulted in significant evolutionary advancement across generations and the profusion of a multitude of differing living organisms. Bodies took on a variety of shapes and functions, sensory receptors matured in capacity and sensitivity, and brains evolved in size, synaptic complexity and intellect.

Ultimately, these advancements resulted in the appearance of what has been described as the most complex 1.36 kilos of matter in the known universe … the human brain.

Associated with this unparalleled complexity was the emergence of the human mind which has the ability to think and feel, the capacity to plan and reflect, and the intellect and interest to ponder its existence and significance ... far in advance of any other known life form.

This remarkable development is driven, without effort or intention, at the level of the non-conscious mind.

It is the natural expression of Reality.

⌣

So, how did your conscious mind develop? And where did your world come from?

To answer these challenging questions let's turn our attention back to the moment of your birth.

As a newborn you were aware but not fully conscious. Your brain was 30% of its full adult size. Billions of neural connections were yet to form. Your senses were present but not fully developed. You were aware of sensory information, but it was largely meaningless. Your world was little more than a shadow.

Yet, in the space of a very few years your world in all its wonder came into existence. From a shadowy world devoid of space and time, it grew in space and time. It was populated with people, things and experiences. It took on meaning and significance, and was coloured with hopes and dreams, but also disappointment and failure.

Let's consider what we know about the development of your world.

At the outset, though, I'd like to remind you that when I use words such as "brain", "neuron" and "synaptic connection" I am referring to non-conscious expressions of Reality which we attempt to understand through the filter of consciousness.

We know that from the moment of birth the brain continues making neural connections. As sensory information is received it is relayed to the brain where it is recorded across a range of developing synaptic connections.

Significantly, while this information can promote the growth of new connections, more often it strengthens existing connections. As fresh sensory information is filtered through existing connections, the neural connection is not only reinforced but a particular way of interpreting that information begins to emerge.

The tracing and retracing of neural connections and repetition of particular interpretations results in the formation of sub-conscious and conscious memory. In effect, memory becomes the basis by which new sensory information is interpreted.

Through this process of building memory upon memory upon memory, information which was meaningless starts to have meaning. Conscious memories start to form out of memories which were otherwise non-conscious. Mere random sensations are transformed into experiences and the picture of an increasingly familiar world starts to emerge.

What you perceive is a product of your collected memories (non-conscious, sub-conscious and conscious). As such, any perception you have is an expression of the entirety of your past history.

～

This conditioning results in the emergence of a seemingly all-encompassing mental image.

While many connections which existed at birth are strengthened through constant reinforcement, many other connections which existed at birth are not reinforced and die off through lack of use.

A serviceable picture emerges through the connections that are strengthened, but at the expense of connections which are neglected. Arguably, the downside of this conditioning process is the loss of potential brain power and associated insight.

Had a less conditioned and more holistic neural network been maintained, a possibly very different mental picture and, indeed, understanding of your world may have resulted.

～

Through this process of strengthening certain connections through reinforcement and losing other connections through neglect, a unique neural circuitry develops.

Quite incredibly this circuitry results in the unique appearance of a world existing in seemingly real space and time and a person – 'you' – who thinks, feels and acts in this world.

This image exists by virtue of neural circuitry. Change that circuitry and you change the appearance of the resulting world. Destroy it and you destroy the associated world.

~

This raises the question, if the mental picture is a product of neural connections, a picture which may be manipulated by changes to those connections, just how 'real' is the mental image of a seemingly real world which emerges?

I guess the first point that we can make is that while the picture may be very convincing, it certainly didn't exist at birth. The original picture you experienced at birth was nothing like the picture you experience now. Instead, the picture that you are now familiar with is a complicated mental interpretation of what would otherwise have been meaningless information. It is an image which resulted from a neural network that developed over time. You could say that the image is a mental sculpture … a product of billions of years of non-conscious conditioning and decades of conscious conditioning.

The second point that we can make is that, notwithstanding the seeming reality of the picture, the only factor that makes your world at all familiar to you is the memory on which it is constructed. If you were to lose the entirety of that sub-conscious and conscious memory right now, then your world which you are currently intimately familiar with would instantly vanish. I suggest that it would then appear very similar to the meaningless sensations you experienced at birth. And if the entirety of the non-conscious memory was lost as well, then only the potential of the Reality would remain.

The third point is that we should not overlook the fact that the entirety of this world – which seems to exist in real space and time – actually only arises in the infinitesimally small gap between neural connections. Without those connections the image wouldn't exist. Even the idea of a conscious world arising in the gaps between neural connections is itself a product of neural circuitry. Without that circuitry, there is no conscious world.

The conclusion must be that the world exists as you experience it. Your world is your experience of it. And that there is no 'real' world that exists beyond that experience.

~

I know that you may struggle with the suggestion that your world depends on neural circuitry and may be tempted to ask, "But, if this is so, how could our interpretation lead us to believe that this world is tangible and real? How can we be so oblivious to the fact that it is just a mental image?"

There is no easy answer to these questions, but it would appear that this mindset is largely due to untested assumptions about what is observed. Certainly, throughout life we have a habit of making false assumptions about what we observe.

As you might be able to recall, as infants our worlds appeared as mental images to which we didn't attribute much continuity. And so, in a game of 'peek-a-boo' we smiled when we saw a face and thought that it vanished when it disappeared behind a cloth. It was only as toddlers that we gained the idea of continuity and realised that the face didn't disappear but was merely hidden from view. By the time we were adults, we came to interpret the mental images we encountered as not only continuous but tangible realities existing independently of us. The illusion was complete.

While this assumption was useful in our personal development and indeed the evolutionary development of mankind, it didn't afford us a complete understanding of the nature and complexity of what we observe.

However, with the insights now available to us we can realise a more holistic perspective. We can comprehend that our worlds are incredibly complex mental images, exhibiting continuity yet being intangible. And we can understand how our worlds amount to a mere interpretation of otherwise meaningless information ... the tracing of a picture where no such picture actually exists. Yes, our respective worlds are an illusion ... but what an incredible illusion.

~

Of course, if your world arises as a product of neural connections and exists in the gaps between them, then your world is undoubtedly a mental phenomenon.

However, I would suggest that the real significance of your world is not so much that it is just a mental phenomenon that appears in your mind but, rather, that it *is* your conscious mind. What you think of as your world is, in fact, your conscious mind. They aren't just intricately interrelated; they are one and the same.

The neural connections which result in the appearance of your conscious mind are the same neural connections which result in the appearance of your world. Those connections don't produce two separate pictures – one your conscious mind and the other your world – but, rather, the same mental picture.

There is no boundary between where your mind starts and where your world ends. Mind is world and world is mind.

~

While your attention may be taken with the appearances which populate your world, they are merely reflective of your mind.

Your world is not only an appearance in mind it depends on the state of your mind.

State of world is the state of mind.

25 Experience makes the person

Over the last few chapters we've considered the appearance of conceptual 'I' and 'not-I', the relationship of mind and matter, the nature of life, the emergence of consciousness, and the appearance of the mental image which is both your conscious mind and your world. And we have noted that all is an expression of the underlying source Reality.

Action may appear to occur at the conscious level, but in fact true action occurs at the non-conscious level. It determines if consciousness emerges, what manifests in consciousness and how that manifestation appears. Actually, anything which appears or occurs in your world is the result of non-conscious functioning. It defines and shapes all without effort or intention.

As for your world, it is your conscious mind. It exists as a series of mental images and is without depth or substance.

In this chapter I would like to turn our attention to a key ingredient of your world ... the emerging person.

You must have observed a new born baby ... seen it look upon its world without comprehension, move its little body without intention and cry as a purely automatic reaction. And I guess that you must have realised that life was once like that for you.

While you have the full use of your body now, it hasn't always been like that. Not all that long ago you too were like that little baby. The movements of your head and limbs were also uncoordinated and amounted to little more than a series of jerky, instinctive and unintentional reflexes. For all intents and purposes, your body was a foreign object. There was no thought or deliberation in anything you did. You cried when you were hungry and slept when you were tired. All happened naturally and unintentionally.

And yet out of this automatic functioning, your body grew in strength, your movements improved in coordination and your actions increased in intentionality.

However, it was not only your body that grew. As a baby your sense of self was just as undeveloped as your newborn body. At birth you didn't have any concepts about yourself; you had no notions about your gender or appearance, and didn't even entertain the thought that you were a person. There was no sense of 'me'.

Yet, automatically and without effort, the person you now think you are emerged.

How did this happen?

As a newborn you had no ideas about yourself but through experience developed into the person you now are. By interacting with your environment, layer upon layer of memory was laid down and sensory information was transformed into experience. With each experience you not only learned how to use your body, but also gained ideas about who you are.

Through those experiences, you learned to call yourself a name and label yourself boy or girl. You came to understand yourself in terms of your relationships with other people, the activities you engaged in, the possessions you owned and the beliefs you maintained. You discovered what you like and don't like, what is and isn't important to you, and what you want to achieve. You became a person, complete with personality, character, habits, ideas and beliefs.

Through repeated exposure to those learned aspects of self, you came to identify with them and believe that you are an autonomous person living life and pursuing your own ends. That is, a real entity blessed with independent existence.

You do so even though everything about the person you think you are exists as a collection of mental images, in the gap between the most delicate of neural connections. If those neural connections are altered, the person is altered. And if the neural connections are severed, the person you think you are vanishes ... completely, wholly, utterly.

~

We might have the idea that the developing person is the subject of experiences, that the experiences happen to the person, but this is a misperception: the developing person is not the subject of experiences but a product of them.

At birth the idea 'me' doesn't exist but, through experience, comes into existence and develops into the person you think you are. Each and every experience not only affects the person, it makes the person.

The person is so dependent on their experiences that they can't be separated from them. Change the experience and you change the person. In the absence of experiences there is absolutely no person ... a body maybe, but no person.

No person exists independently of their experiences. Experiences are central to the person you are today.

⁓

Even though you may feel very confident about being the person you think you are, it would not take too many twists of fate to affect that person deeply, profoundly and irrevocably.

What experiences would it take for you?

Financial ruin? Relationship failure? Traumatic injury? The imminent prospect of death? Death? Or just the realisation that the person you've always thought you are is actually just a mental image resulting from non-conscious processes, existing in the gap between neural connections.

＿

Any person is only as durable as the experiences on which it is based.

You may be comfortable with the mental image you currently have about yourself, but are you just that mental image? Are you a mental image at all?

What are you in the absence of mental images? What are you?

＿

We will be exploring the depths of what you are in much greater detail than this brief introduction, but first we need to consider significant aspects of the developing person's psyche and in so doing some of the obstacles that may prevent self-realisation.

26 The love to be

In this chapter I'd like to consider the developing psyche of the person and in particular the emergence of love and the emotions of fear and desire.

I think that the best place to commence our examination of these seemingly diverse characteristics is the moment of birth.

⁓

At birth the new born infant does not have a thought in its mind and yet its instinct to survive is fully formed. Sure, it is helpless, it can't fend for itself and doesn't even know what its needs are and yet its limited abilities are exactly what it needs to survive. When hungry or in pain it spontaneously screams; there is no conscious thought, yet it results in the care and attention necessary for its survival.

This baby is born with the instinct to survive. At this early stage it can't be said to be a desire to live or a fear of dying, but nevertheless there is an undeniable instinctive non-conscious urge to survive.

Shortly thereafter the infant becomes aware of its body … consciousness starts to dawn. And the unarticulated sense 'I am' is expressed as 'I love to be'. The child may not be consciously aware that they love to be, but nevertheless, there is increasing evidence of this love in the pattern of their behaviour. Fears about threats to the wellbeing of their body start to emerge, as does their conscious desire to be safe, secure and protected. These are symptomatic of the increasingly conscious desire to live and fear of dying.

As the child grows in confidence and security, this love to be is extended beyond the 'physical' body to incorporate concepts of '**me**' and '**mine**'.

—

'**Me**' is the idea of self that develops through life. It results from impressions gathered through experiences. The experiences may result from enjoyable or traumatic events. The associated impressions may be negative or positive, relate to appearance, ability, character, position in society or any other trait whether inherited or learned.

While some impressions form in isolation, many arise from comparisons with other people or from the judgements of others.

Crucially, the self-image exists as a mental image; it represents a learned aspect of self and is subject to change. It is a natural expression of the environment as perceived.

—

Just as love for the body is expressed as a combination of desire and fear, so is the love for 'me'. There is the desire that the 'me' will flourish, achieve and succeed ... but also the fear that the 'me' will disappoint, flounder or fail.

The result is that insecurity is inevitable. Either a person will feel inadequate, believing 'I'm not good enough' or 'no one could love me', or they fear that threats to their self-image may render them inadequate. As such, even if successful, the person could still fear failure and, despite acceptance, fear rejection.

~

'**Mine**' are the possessions, people and principles which are associated with 'me'. They are considered necessary to appease the love for 'me'.

And just as the love for 'me' is expressed as fear and desire, so is the love for 'mine'. A person desires to protect, control and maximise what is 'mine' but fears the lack, loss and demise of 'mine'.

And like the love of 'me', the love of 'mine' also produces inadequacy. Either a person will desire what they don't have or fear losing what they do have.

~

Whereas love may be expressed as a desire to protect body, 'me' and 'mine' and a fear of harm to body, 'me' and 'mine', it may also be expressed as the preferences of like and dislike, and the passions of love and hate.

Every sensation or experience that is encountered in life is categorised as pleasant, unpleasant or neither pleasant nor unpleasant. The pleasant and unpleasant experiences make a particular impression and a unique pattern of likes and dislikes emerges.

These likes and dislikes have a powerful effect on behaviour, especially when those likes and dislikes take shape as the passions of love and hate. The person gravitates towards experiences which are pleasant and avoids experiences which are unpleasant, resulting in a particular course of behaviour.

There is a dynamic movement from less to more favourable conditions.

—

Significantly, this pattern of behaviour is not a novel occurrence confined to humans or other animals and beings. Instead, it is reflected at every stage of evolutionary development.

The non-conscious movement from less to more favourable conditions results in the emergence of atoms and elements, suns and galaxies, and indeed the appearance of order and stability at every scale and degree of complexity in the universe.

Everything, including human behaviour, is shaped by non-conscious forces of attraction and repulsion.

Indeed, life is shaped by love. Life is love in action.

—

Interestingly, although humans instinctively gravitate towards what they find immediately gratifying, because of higher intellect and conditioning, they also learn to delay gratification.

The result is that people will be prepared to sacrifice immediate satisfaction for the promise of greater future rewards and will willingly endure less pleasant tasks (such as work) for future enjoyment (such as holidays).

By gravitating towards a combination of immediate pleasures and longer term goals, the person hopes to realise happiness, safeguard against unhappiness, and live the best life they can.

—

The significance of this force in a person's life cannot be overstated.

Their life becomes a process of shuttling between the boundaries of fear and desire: between what must be achieved and what must be avoided.

Fear and desire are the warp and weft of human existence. Yet ... the essence is love.

—

It is love which is the prime motivator of all activities. It is love which fuels the desire to succeed, be happy and live an enjoyable life, but also the fear of being unhappy, rejected and a failure.

Out of love the person not only creates, protects and nurtures, but also destroys, attacks and hates. Out of love a person can do the most lovable and love worthy things, but also the most vile and hateful.

Every action has love at its root. The action may be magnanimous and wise or selfish and misguided, but love is the motivating factor.

And what should not be forgotten is that love in all its guises is the love to be. As such, even the love we have for others is actually an expression of the love we have for ourselves.

Ultimately though, all these seemingly diverse feelings and emotions are conscious expressions of the non-conscious instinct to survive.

~

Think about the role of love in your life.

Love expressed as fear and desire has moulded your actions, crafted your self-image, shaped your relationship with world, and defined the person you think you are now.

Change the fear and desire and you change everything ... actions, world, self-image and person.

Eliminate the fear and desire ... and only pure love remains.

Love is all.

27 Happiness is natural

Out of self-love you want to feel fulfilled and secure, but above all you want to be happy.

Continuing with our exploration of the human psyche, I'd like to turn our attention to happiness.

What is happiness? How does it arise? And why is it so elusive?

⁓

I think that we can safely make the point that prior to the appearance of consciousness there were no emotions or feelings. All non-conscious functioning transpired in serene peacefulness. Atoms formed and galaxies were devoured without the slightest emotional disturbance.

In consciousness this serenity is expressed as happiness. Happiness is the sensation of deep abiding peace. It is an intrinsic aspect of consciousness. While consciousness is present, so is happiness.

As a young infant happiness was your natural state. In adults it is best described as, "I don't want or need anything. I have no worries or concerns. I am full and complete." It is a feeling of complete tranquillity and security.

Happiness isn't a product of experiences and doesn't depend on situations. It doesn't disappear through lack of stimulation. In fact, it doesn't change. Instead, it is more like the sun which shines regardless of whether it is day or night. It underpins all experiences, whether pleasant or not. And regardless of what happens, it knows no darkness.

Certainly, the more you are aware of this happiness, the happier you will be. However, while this happiness is always available, it is often overlooked.

~

Although this core happiness is ever-present, it is also subtle and so doesn't grab the attention of the developing child. Instead as a child, your attention was attracted by experiences which excite and interest ... the prized toys, curious animals, the attentive people. You enjoyed these stimulating encounters and looked forward to repeating them.

These pleasurable experiences not only captivated your attention, they came to dominate your outlook ... and, in the process, the subtle serenity of the core happiness was overlooked.

These early tendencies were perpetuated and pleasurable experiences – usually regarding possessions, people or other interests – continued capturing your attention. These pleasures took on a significant role in your life at the expense of the core happiness.

The result is that while you may be very familiar with the sensation of pleasure, you may be quite ignorant of the exquisite beauty of core happiness. You may assume that pleasure is the only form of happiness and may even believe that core happiness doesn't exist. As such, it isn't surprising if you are dependent on pleasure for happiness.

~

Pleasure, of course, is a type of happiness. You could even say that it is an expression of happiness ... or a natural development of non-conscious serene peacefulness.

There are, however, several crucial differences between core happiness and pleasure:

- Core happiness and pleasure are both products of consciousness; however, while happiness only relies on consciousness, pleasure additionally relies on a particular relationship between 'me' and 'mine'.

- While both happiness and pleasure are agreeable sensations, happiness is expressed as just one sensation (abiding peace) whereas pleasure is expressed in a multitude of sensations (amusement, delight, satisfaction).

- Even though pleasure may be intensely enjoyable and deeply rewarding, it is a temporary sensation. Arising from experiences which come and go, so does the resulting pleasure. In contrast, happiness doesn't vary.

- While pleasure may be very enjoyable, it is susceptible to the most minor of disappointments. Unlike happiness, even the most gratifying pleasure can vanish with just the hint of bad news.

- It is destructive to seek endless pleasure. Over-reliance on pleasure can lead to addiction to anything from food to money … and when taken to excess can not only be devastating to the person but also the planet. In contrast, core happiness cannot cause harm.

- Pleasure can only offer a superficial type of happiness. It can't provide the deep or lasting sense of peace, contentment or fulfilment … which is the experience of core happiness. Instead, when pleasure departs it leaves the person wanting more.

- Crucially, pleasure cannot result in happiness. Sights and sounds may give pleasure, but never happiness. To experience happiness it must be experienced directly.

While pleasure may result from a given situation; happiness is what is brought to the situation.

~

If you have spent your life focusing on pleasure you will only be familiar with a happiness that is dependent on external factors. That dependence ensures a happiness which is both temporary and vulnerable.

You will not be aware of core happiness which is permanent and secure.

~

While the singular reliance on pleasure may create the belief that it is necessary to have and do things to be happy, in fact, the opposite is true.

Happiness can't be bought, earned or achieved. Neither can it result from relationships with other people. It can't be realised through pursuing interests. It isn't a product of pleasure. Yet, happiness is readily available. It only requires conscious awareness.

The only reason why it may be elusive is the means of securing it. Seeking happiness through pleasure obscures the sense of wholeness and completeness that people most want in life.

If you are satisfied with pleasure, genuine happiness must remain elusive.

~

Happiness is freedom from having to have and do things.

For happiness, the journey is inward, not outward.

Once happiness is realised, nothing is the same again. It is a life changing experience for anyone.

28 The 'good' life

Over the last few chapters we have traced the appearance of consciousness, love and happiness and have noted that they are conscious expressions of the non-conscious mind.

We have further noted that the person is a product of conditioning forces and gravitates toward a combination of culturally determined longer term goals and immediate pleasures.

In modern western society, these factors conspire to produce an 'ideal' where the person pursues financial gain, forms meaningful relationships, purchases a house, raises a family, accumulates possessions and enjoys their interests.

This 'good' life is broadly considered best for the individual and, not coincidentally, the society.

~

While this approach may be aimed at enriching the lives of people and may be considered the ideal by western society, it is not without its problems.

The daily grind of life – work, pay bills and raise a family – is a stressful experience.

- The promise of the 'good' life is no promise of a good life. Dysfunction in the family home, stress in the work place, and financial pressure are not uncommon experiences.

- The so called 'good' life offers little protection against painful experiences, such as the death of loved ones. And even in the course of a normal day, the person remains susceptible to a range of unpleasant feelings, such as agitation, frustration, annoyance, sadness, boredom, anger, distress, worry and loneliness.

- The 'good' life is not necessarily as satisfying as expected. Even if a person is blessed with a loving family, career success and financial security, they may still have the nagging sense that something is missing in their life.

~

Given the stressfulness of pursuing the 'good' life, the person often needs distraction and will look for relief in a range of pleasurable activities, which could include coffee, alcohol, retail therapy, exercise, comfort food, sex, TV, drugs, annual holidays.

While the favoured activity is a welcome diversion and does take the person's mind off their stresses, the relief is only temporary. When the person re-engages with the daily grind, the sense of pleasure quickly fades and the stresses inherent in the pursuit of the 'good' life surface again.

Once more the person needs the escape afforded by their usual pleasures, they feel better for a while but the same stresses start to emerge.

This cycle of working to achieve longer term goals but then needing the distraction of shorter term pleasures becomes habitual.

⌐

I would suggest that the reason why a person pursues a combination of longer term goals and shorter term pleasures is because they want to be happy.

Certainly, this desire to be happy is natural. However, I would also make the point that a less obvious aspect of this desire is that it masks an underlying level of discontent. By this I mean that the underlying reason why a person desires the 'good' life is because they aren't entirely happy in the first place. Arguably, if they were, there would be no discontent and no corresponding desire to either pursue the 'good' life or seek relief from the pursuit through pleasure.

It is a significant observation that a person's pursuit of either the 'good' life or pleasure is indicative of unhappiness at some level. However, perhaps even more telling is the fact that neither the 'good' life nor the pleasures they pursue actually eradicates the underlying unhappiness.

~

This represents a very general overview of the approach that people adopt in western society and the situation in which you may find yourself.

While I don't necessarily want to challenge the value of this approach, I would suggest that the singular pursuit of the 'good' life may result in two undesirable consequences.

First it may bind the person to unnecessary unhappiness. And, second, it may blind them to a richer experience of life.

~

As a person pursues the 'good' life, they inevitably experience unhappiness ... whether arising from stress or setback. While this unhappiness may be viewed as a necessary sacrifice for longer term benefits, it is of greater concern if it is assumed that the unhappiness is in any way inevitable.

With this assumption, the person, out of fear of realising greater unhappiness, may continue to pursue a less than satisfactory existence.

While this logic may be highly persuasive, it does, however, overlook a very significant consideration. It may be the case that unhappiness is not inevitable and may actually be symptomatic of the pursuit of the 'good' life. That pursuit may actually create, perpetuate and entrench unnecessary unhappiness.

If this is the case, then rather than seek escape though the standard combination of longer term goals and immediate pleasures, it may be more appropriate to question the appropriateness of the pursuit and the associated understanding, beliefs and behaviours.

This is not to say that a person would have to relinquish family, work, money or any of the other usual symbols of happiness. To the contrary, it may merely require a reappraisal of the role of unhappiness and how they respond to it.

With regard to the second point, the focus on the 'good' life may result in more limited life experiences.

This is not to say that the person who focuses on family, work and money will be miserable. Nor is it to say that they won't have had many enjoyable and worthwhile experiences. To the contrary, they may well have experienced many memorable moments, amounting to what they consider a rich life.

However, if a person is only familiar with passing pleasure, they will be ignorant of the greatest experience of all … lasting (core) happiness.

This lasting happiness is the happiness which everyone desires but is often absent in people's lives.

To realise this happiness, a more holistic approach to life is needed rather than the singular pursuit of the 'good' life though money, work, family or other pleasurable experiences.

⁓

So, we're left with a situation where, because of what society says, a person may feel that they have to form relationships, acquire possessions and pursue experiences to be happy.

Yet, even if they are diligent and do all that is expected of them, the very pursuit of this happiness may result in stress and unhappiness … so much so that they need to take a break from the pursuit … regularly.

If the person is determined to persist in the pursuit and is favoured with good fortune, they may be feted with love, wealth and status. However, even when they think they've arrived at their goal, they realise that they still haven't achieved what they want most of all ... lasting happiness.

Despite all their efforts and achievements, there is a shadow of unhappiness which they haven't been able to shake.

While that unhappiness remains, no matter what the person does, where they go or what they have, genuine happiness will remain elusive. They will not feel whole and complete.

~

I would, however, like to finish this chapter by noting that lasting happiness is available now.

While it can't be experienced by pursuing the pleasures on offer in the 'good' life, it can be realised through freedom from unhappiness.

By learning from the lessons that unhappiness has to teach, true happiness is revealed.

29 Breaking the cycle

In the last chapter we considered the pursuit of the 'good' life through family, work, money and possessions. We noted that the pursuit arises in response to a level of discontent but also produces further discontent. Typically that discontent is appeased through a combination of longer term goals and shorter term pleasures.

While the discontent may be assuaged temporarily, because the approach is focused on escaping the discontent as opposed to dealing with it, the underlying discontent is never fully addressed, allowing it to reoccur throughout a person's life. As a result lasting happiness is not a common experience.

While there are variations in the approach – a greater focus on longer term goals as opposed to immediate pleasures, on money as opposed to family, or on work as opposed to personal interests – they all share one characteristic in common. They all focus on getting more ... more love, more pleasure, more possessions, more respect.

This particular reliance on 'more' is a product of conditioning and has arisen through cultural and social forces which developed over many years.

Crucially though, while this need for 'more' is predominant in modern western culture, it is not the only approach.

In this chapter we will consider how people come to break the cycle they have been conditioned to pursue.

~

Typically, a person engages in the pursuit of 'more' just as they have been taught and just like everyone else.

For most people this approach is never seriously questioned. Even if the person experiences unfulfilling work, a dysfunctional relationship, financial difficulties or resorts to ultimately detrimental pleasures, they still don't abandon their reliance on 'more'. While the circumstance may change, their approach does not. 'More' is all they know and want.

There are others, though, who may enjoy the experience of 'more' but come to realise that it is not totally satisfactory. They will have the sense that something is missing and that they don't feel full and complete; that there is a 'hole' if their life which hasn't been filled. However, while they may be open to exploring what else life has to offer, they won't be prepared to abandon their attachment to 'more'. They live in hope that one day 'more' will be enough.

Then there are those few other people who abandon their reliance on 'more'. They often experience an epiphany which allows them to see through their conditioned habits and reactions. They recognise that 'more' is never enough and have the courage to discover a better way.

In very rare cases this epiphany may be brought about by instinctive wisdom or from heeding wise advice.

Mostly though, the epiphany is brought about by a life crisis. While many people struggle with the weight of their suffering and be unable to move beyond, there are others who find unexpected strength in the midst of their adversity and experience the epiphany which changes their life.

The epiphany may be sparked by a slow build-up of discontent which peaks in overwhelming disillusionment or, alternatively, can result from a major shock in the form of personal hardship, illness or tragedy. Whatever the particular chain of events, it results in a deep and pervading sense of unhappiness which awakens the person to the plight of their situation and the futility of life as they have been living it.

This deep unhappiness won't be denied or silenced, and can't be papered over by the continued pursuit of 'more'.

It demands a fundamental re-evaluation of where their life is heading and what they want out of it.

Suffering lights the flame of awareness.

~

People who experience this level of unhappiness may ask soul-searching questions, such as: Why do I feel so unhappy? What am I doing wrong in my life? What changes must I make?

When the questions are heartfelt and the person truly wants an answer, the response is forthcoming.

They realise that the unhappiness they are experiencing is an amplified version of the unhappiness that has haunted them throughout their life. They realise that any attempt to escape that unhappiness through 'more' not only fails to resolve their situation but makes things worse. They realise that the reliance on 'more' was never the solution; it was always a big part of the problem. They realise that they must attend to their unhappiness. They realise their need to take responsibility.

The person clearly perceives the need to change their goals, attitudes and priorities. And they do.

~

In reading these words, you will know where you fit.

Either your unhappiness is an overwhelming burden for you or it isn't. Either you want to do something about it or you don't. Either you are motivated to learn or you aren't.

Your attitude to unhappiness both forges your motivation to learn and steels your determination to succeed. If you have the strong desire to be free of unhappiness, you can realise happiness beyond imagination.

~

Speaking from my own experience, unhappiness had some very profound lessons for me.

I had been going through a challenging patch in my life and because of situations seemingly out of my control found myself desperately unhappy. My situation was so dire that it seemed as though my mind had shattered into a million pieces. I thought that I could never put those pieces together again.

Despite the seeming hopelessness, I instinctively knew I had to take responsibility for my situation and that significant changes were necessary. I questioned all aspects of my life and enquired into the cause of my unhappiness.

It came as a shock to me to realise that my unhappiness was due to my desires to be somewhere else, doing something different … in other words, my desire for 'more'. Rather than the situation, it was my fight against the situation that fuelled my unhappiness.

I realised that if I was to find any relief that a new approach was necessary. Rather than pursue 'more' I needed to bring my attention to what I wanted to escape from. And rather than fight the situation I had to learn from it.

This realisation gave me some peace, which deepened when I started to act on the insight.

Then a few days later an incredible event occurred. I can recall experiencing an empty sensation in my chest. However, rather than ignore or try to escape from the sensation I was calmly indifferent and observed it from a distance. I was aware but free. To my surprise it diminished and soon dissolved.

Remarkably, I then experienced the most beautiful serenity, the like of which I had never experienced before, wash throughout my body. Words cannot adequately capture the experience, but I was one and all. I found myself feeling serenely happy for the first time.

I knew that there was nothing more that I wanted in my life than this happiness. I knew that this happiness lay within and wasn't a product of 'more'. I knew that I had awakened to a deeper way of being.

This epiphany was a pivotal moment in my life. Happiness had exploded into my life and nothing would ever be the same again.

⁓

My personal experiences may be of little interest to you, but the insight it affords is that beneath whatever unhappiness you experience lies an exquisite happiness, the like of which you can't imagine.

However, it cannot be discovered through pursuing 'more' of anything. Instead, the happiness you seek lies within. To struggle for 'more' is to settle for less.

Turn your attention from what you think you need and understand why you think you need it. Be aware of the discontent which fuels your need for 'more'.

Realise that deepest vulnerability from which you desperately want to escape ... and accept it. Only then can you know happiness.

That feeling of wholeness and completeness – which is genuine happiness – is all you can wish. It is the joy you have been searching for all your life.

It is not 'more'; it is enough ... it is more than enough.

30 You are the happiness you seek

In the previous chapter we noted that deep unhappiness can bring about an epiphany whereby the person can see through their conditioned patterns of living. This insight can shift their focus beyond the pursuit of 'more' so that they are attuned to the lessons that life has to teach them.

This broadening of focus can be described as the birth of spirituality in the person's life.

While this spiritual dimension may incorporate a belief in divinities (including associated worship and prayers), use of spiritual paraphernalia and reliance on the teachings of others, these are not the only approaches.

My personal experience of spirituality was quite different. While I was open-minded to these various approaches, I found that I was not drawn to them. I didn't feel the need to believe in a deity and had little use of spiritual supports.

Instead, it was important to me that my spirituality grew out of my own direct experience. While I was amenable to listening to what others said, I didn't want to just rely on their words. While I was open to guidance, I was keen to explore my spirituality for myself.

〜

If I were to analyse my spiritual practice I would say that it comprised two basic approaches. One was a focus on unhappiness and the other was a focus on happiness.

When I experienced unhappiness, I wouldn't avoid the sensation but instead appreciated it as an opportunity to learn. By tracing the unhappiness to its core I would inevitably uncover an underlying assumption, attachment, belief or expectation about what should or should not happen. Having identified that cause, I could then address the unhappiness.

I discovered that the more I relinquished detrimental thought patterns, the less unhappiness I experienced. I continued focusing on any unhappiness that arose until it became a very rare experience. Ultimately, it ceased altogether.

The other aspect of my practice was to focus on happiness. While I, like everyone else, enjoyed pleasurable experiences, I was aware of the more subtle experience of genuine happiness. In meditation I would explore this happiness by bringing my attention to the body and, during my daily life, I would feel the happiness glowing from within. This bliss of conscious awareness shined brightly in my life and it became the abiding reality of my existence.

~

While these dual approaches undoubtedly had significant beneficial effects on my enjoyment of life, the real value was its effect on my ego ... that is, my ideas of 'me' and my attachment to 'mine'.

As my attention was firmly focused on happiness and unhappiness, it became apparent that much of what I had learned in life had to be unlearned. What I clung to had to be surrendered. What I resisted had to be accepted. And what I thought was indispensable had to be recognised as dispensable.

With each lesson, the firm grip of my ego lessened.

While this process certainly did reveal the happiness underpinning pleasure and suffering, and the love laying beneath fear and desire, far more crucially it directed me to the self at the root of the self-image.

Ultimately this practice led to self-realisation, which is the greatest life-changing transformation that can be experienced.

Please don't think that I am exaggerating.

Following self-realisation, everything is perceived in a different and wonderful light. There is an ease to life and things fall into place as they should and must. You live the life you love. Happiness is your reality: unhappiness is a distant memory.

In my view, there is nothing more you can wish for.

~

The whole purpose of this book is to guide you on your spiritual journey to the direct realisation of self.

Having questioned, in the first part of the book, many assumptions that you may have maintained about the nature of your world, we will now question mistaken assumptions you may have about self.

In the process of exploring these mistaken assumptions, you will be encouraged to become aware of the role of unhappiness in your life and the lessons it can teach you. And through extensive practical exercises you will be encouraged to stabilise in genuine happiness.

Ultimately, as a result of the responsibility you take, the accompanying insights you experience and the mistaken assumptions you relinquish, the self will be revealed.

~

Before we continue with our exploration of the self, I would like to share an analogy which may in some way help explain the journey you are about to embark upon.

The analogy is that of a rock sitting in the middle of a powerful river. As the rock is pounded by the river, it resists the river's relentless flow. Eventually the rock gives way to the might of the river and is dissolved. Then, only the inexorable river remains.

The ego is like the rock. During the course of life the ego is pounded by the river of life. In order to survive these challenges it has to be stubborn and resist the threats that life presents. In so doing, the ego suffers stress and unhappiness is inevitable.

While you identify with your ego, you will fiercely resist relinquishing your assumptions about 'me' and your attachments to 'mine': to do so would be death and destruction. You will fight for your identity as the ego and may have little interest in knowing yourself as anything other than the rock.

This situation can last indefinitely; however, a particular combination of challenging life experiences (or just wisdom) can bring your attention to the ego and cause you to recognise that your ego – or more particularly your desire to protect the ego – is actually the problem. With this awareness, you let go and the friction of life wears the ego away. Then only the river remains.

The realisation then dawns that your reality was never the problematic ego-rock, but rather the living and vibrant river. It may take years or even generations, but it can just as easily happen now.

As the river, there is no need to preserve a learned identity; you simply flow. You are free and in harmony with whatever is encountered. Without false ideas there is no resistance or unhappiness. There is just the happiness of self. Nothing can make you happier than you already are.

~

The goal of the spiritual journey is to lead you back to the self.

If you are to realise genuine happiness, then don't look for refuge in the ego or any of your attachments. They are the problem. Rather, realise what you are. Be diligent, learn from happiness and unhappiness, and distinguish the self-image from the reality of the self.

The happiness that you want can only come from self-realisation. Only the full realisation of what you are eternally, perennially and changelessly can give the sense of fullness and completeness that you most desire.

Self is what you want and what you need. Once your true identity is realised your search is over. You are the happiness you seek.

True happiness is not what you gain but that vastness you have never lost. The realisation of self is what is missing in your life.

⌣

The fact that you are is clear ... now you just need to realise what you are.

Delay is a waste of time, all else a distraction.

31 What are you?

Consider yourself looking up at the immensity of a starry night. Each pinprick of light is a distant sun whose light has travelled from out of the distant reaches of time and space to meet you. You are struck by its seeming vastness and antiquity.

This ancient expanse gave birth to your body and brain, and even the consciousness which lights your world. Yet this spectacle only exists as a mental picture in your mind. This image exists by virtue of your eyes and brain; it is your perception. Without your consciousness there is Reality but not your perception of it. And without your perception the image of that starry sky doesn't exist.

On the one hand, stars give birth to the appearance of consciousness and, on the other, consciousness gives birth to the appearance of stars.

But, what are you in this mix? Stardust? Consciousness? Both? Or perhaps neither?

⁓

For the remainder of this book we are going to focus on the reality of what you are. Step by step we will peel back the layers of self-image to reveal the self.

We will go beyond the changing appearance of body, beyond the momentary flashes of thought and feeling, and even beyond the sense of being which lights everything in your world.

Journeying to the limits of conceptual knowledge, you will be invited to realise, as your direct experience, the incomprehensible immensity of your reality.

With sincere desire you will come to the startling realisation of what you are.

~

What do we know about 'you'?

Well, I guess that it's easy to think of yourself as a person: an individual with unique hopes and ambitions; a human being which was born and will die; a fleeting speck in a vast universe; an otherwise inconsequential combination of atoms.

This is certainly the view propounded by mainstream culture. However, even though you may agree with this perspective and may even think that it is an obvious observation, it is, nevertheless, an assumption.

It is an assumption which overlooks the pivotal role that you play in your world.

When I use the word 'pivotal' I mean it in the greatest sense possible. Everything that happens in your world happens to you. Every sensation that exists in your world is your sensation. Every perception is your perception. Every experience is your experience. Every understanding is your understanding.

You play such a pivotal role that your world revolves around you. Everything in your world points to the fact of 'you' at its centre.

You are so much at its centre that you define seemingly universal concepts of 'here' and 'now'. Wherever you are it is always 'here'. Whenever you are it is always 'now'. Without trying, you define here and now just by being.

What is that 'you' which can do that?

~

And, of course, the entirety of your seemingly vast world is cradled in the cup of your consciousness.

Through your conscious perception you effortlessly transform non-sensation into sensation, non-experience into experience, non-understanding into understanding. You create where there was no taste, sound where there wasn't even silence and thought and feeling where there was none.

And because of what you are your world appears as you perceive it. It is shaped by your senses, moulded by your interpretation, and seems as real as you judge it to be. Change your perception and your world changes with it.

To say that your world appears to you and only you is such a great understatement. Everything in your world not only appears to you ... it is entirely dependent on you. It only exists because of you.

If you are not, nothing in your world can be. Without you, your world does not exist. Without you it cannot exist.

⌐

Your world doesn't just exist because of you. You are its source. Every sensation, every experience, everything comes from you.

Your world is an expression of what you are: a reflection of 'you'.

⌐

It is easy to marvel at the incredible sights and sounds you experience in life, but the greatest marvel of all isn't any of these mental appearances. It is you!

The real significance of anything and everything is the fact that you are.

Just by being you make everything in your world possible. That is truly incredible!

⌐

The point that I would like you to take away from this chapter is that whatever you are is much more than what you have assumed yourself to be.

I would ask you to be sufficiently open minded to at least consider that what you are may not be a person or an individual, and that your reality may not have been born and may not even die.

While you may think that you are a fleeting speck in a vast universe, it may actually be the other way around. The universe may actually be a fleeting speck in the wonder of what you are.

⌐

Certainly, every sensation, experience and appearance points to you ... but just what are you?

32 What is not Who

Before we can start our exploration of your reality, it is necessary to understand what we actually mean when we ask '*what* are you?'

I guess for most people it may seem that there isn't much difference between the questions 'who are you?' and 'what are you?' They might even seem interchangeable. However, there is a profound distinction.

The question 'what are you?' can't be answered by using a description of who you are.

In this chapter we will consider the respective differences and relationships between 'who' and 'what'. This will not only be useful in indicating the gulf that lies between the two, but more pertinently will be useful in demonstrating what we mean by the question 'what am I?'

⁓

Let me start by making the comment that if I were to ask, 'Who are you?' you could quite sensibly answer by stating your name and age. However, while those details are clearly descriptors of 'who you are' they don't go to the heart of 'what you are'. What you are is not a word or number.

Similarly, while details of nationality, social status and the role you perform in society may be intrinsic to 'who you are', the essence of 'what you are' isn't captured by those social categories.

And although your relationships to other people (e.g. daughter, partner, father) may be another measure of 'who you are', 'what you are' is not any of those relationships. You can have those relationships but you aren't a relationship.

I know that there are many people who like to categorise themselves in terms of the possessions they own, but again this issue only goes to an aspect of 'who' they are. A person can own possessions but what you are isn't determined by the possessions you own.

Undoubtedly, 'who you are' has a history of experiences which is shaped by them and is a product of them, but 'what you are' isn't any of those experiences. They happen to you but you aren't an experience.

And during the course of a life, 'who you are' amasses a variety of I like this-es and I don't like that-s, I believe this-es and I hope for that-s, I think this-es and I feel that-s ... but 'what you are' is distinct from all of those personal preferences.

~

If we try to analyse the differences, I think that we can make the comment that 'who you are' is a product of external relationships ... with the people you know, the things you experience, the values you have learned and what you have come to enjoy. In contrast, 'what you are' isn't a product of any relationships. Instead those relationships are made possible because of what you are.

In other words, while 'who you are' is shaped by your life experiences, 'what you are' makes those experiences possible, but isn't shaped by them ... regardless of how intrinsic, significant or important they might seem.

In this regard, 'who you are' represents conditioned aspects of self, while 'what you are' is completely unconditioned.

~

We can also note that while 'who you are' changes with the passing of major life events ... such as the birth of a child, retirement or physical impairment ... it also changes, more subtly, with each and every experience. 'Who you are' is different now from 5 minutes ago, let alone 20 years ago.

On the other hand, 'what you are' doesn't change. You are 'what you are' before any experience, during any experience and after every experience.

'What you are' underpins all changing versions of 'who you are'. Indeed, 'what you are' creates the sense of being the same though every aspect of 'who you are' has changed.

~

Further, 'who you are' is a product of consciousness and only exists in memory. Without memory no aspect of 'who you are' can exist.

In contrast, 'what you are' isn't a product of consciousness and doesn't rely on memory. You are 'what you are' even if you aren't conscious and have no recollection. 'What you are' doesn't depend on memory or even consciousness.

—

Crucially, we can observe that 'what you are' is the essence of 'who you are'. It makes all the changing permutations of 'who you are' possible. It exists in the gaps between those different permutations. Yet intriguingly, even in the absence of those permutations, you are 'what you are'.

'Who you are' is entirely dependent on 'what you are', but 'what you are' is absolutely independent of 'who you are'.

—

I hope that this discussion helps to clarify the differences between 'who' and 'what' you are. But more than that I hope that it gives you a clear understanding of what is meant by the question 'what am I?'.

It should be clear that while a person tries to understand what they are in terms of their relationships, experiences and memories … they cannot realise what they are.

If a person only knows who they are, they cannot know what they are.

'What am I?' is a very different question from 'Who am I?'

～

'Who you are' is superficial and fleeting. 'What you are' is deep and permanent.

'Who you are' is limited and lacking. 'What you are' is whole and complete.

～

Of course, this does raise a very interesting issue ... if 'who are you' is a reflection of 'what you are' but not actually a measure of 'what you are' ... just what are you?

This intriguing question is the focus of the remainder of this book ... *what* are you ... exactly?

33 What you are is known, just not realised

Having made the distinction between the import of 'who' and 'what' you are, many people would respond to the question 'what are you?' by answering "a human being", "a carbon based life form", "a soul" or "a spirit". While others may claim that given the mysteries of the self it is impossible to ever know what they are.

My take is different to both these types of responses. I would not answer the question 'what are you?' by recourse to any type of classification, yet neither would I agree that it is impossible to know what you are.

Instead, in my experience 'what you are' can be realised, but it is unlike any other form of knowledge. It can't be grasped as a concept, it can't be experienced as a sensation and it can't be realised as a feeling. And yet you can realise 'what you are'.

~

Self-realisation is different from all other understanding because you don't need to do, achieve, acquire, learn or become anything ... you just need to realise what you already are.

There is nothing which can make you more like what you are or bring you closer to the reality of self.

What you are hasn't been lost, so it can't be found.

You already are what you are. You just need to realise what you are.

~

Crucially, no special gift, miracle or divine revelation is necessary, nor are years of hard work, penance, worship or even meditation.

The only prerequisite is a deep desire to realise.

With that desire self-realisation is inevitable. There is nothing more natural than realising what you are.

~

This is not to say that you won't encounter challenges along your journey. You will. However, those challenges don't relate to what you have to gain but what you have to let go.

And what do you need to let go? Nothing more than attachment to mistaken habits of thinking. Only mistaken assumptions prevent self-realisation.

I can promise you that at this very instant the only obstacle you face with regard to self-realisation are mental habits of thinking

.

~

In the first part of the book we identified the first major mental habit preventing self-realisation ... namely, the assumption that your world is an independently existing tangible reality.

If you have been able to work on relinquishing this belief, then you are significantly closer to self-realisation.

The second major mental habit which we will now address is the mistaken assumption that you are what, in fact, you cannot be. If you cling to even the slightest incorrect idea about what you are, it can act as an obstacle and prevent self-realisation.

Only by relinquishing all incorrect ideas can your reality be apperceived. The focus is on letting go.

~

As such, over the next several chapters our emphasis will be on identifying the obstacles to self-realisation ... the false assumptions about what you are.

If you can identify those assumptions and recognise them as mistaken, they will dissolve naturally.

In the absence of those obstacles, the mind is flooded with the clear light of perception. In that clarity the realisation of what you are can dawn.

~

Freedom from self-misunderstanding is not only necessary, it is sufficient. No further understanding is necessary. When the mind is clear you are revealed.

What you are is not what you have assumed or expected. Yet, without doubt you know what you are. You know it now, you have known it all your life ... you just haven't realised it ... yet.

You only need to realise.

⌒

For self-realisation the stress is on the right conditions ... cease all misunderstanding.

Realise what you are not ... deeply, wholly, completely.

What aren't you?

34 You are not the body

If there is one thing that a person identifies with it is their body.

The body is so crucial to a person's existence that they couldn't imagine life without it. Without the body they wouldn't be able to sense or experience anything, and life as they know it would not be possible.

The body is undoubtedly a significant aspect of anyone's existence. But does that mean that you are the body?

In this chapter we will consider whether you could be the body.

While your body may have appeared to be new at birth, it was actually billions of years old. The elements which comprise your body were formed in the cauldron of space and predate the formation of the earth and the sun.

From the perspective of the modern western mind, the hydrogen atoms emerged during the early formation of the universe. The carbon which is the structural base of your body was cooked in stars (along with oxygen) while the iron which makes your blood red was formed in the dying moments of gigantic stars. And the trace-element, zinc, was produced during supernovas.

Even though your infant body seemed new, its genesis actually stretched the length and breadth of the universe. Your body's development encapsulates the development of the universe. The building blocks of your body are the building blocks of the universe.

As such, if you are the body ... then by implication you are not only ancient stardust, you are the building blocks of the universe.

⁓

While the elements of your body are billions of years old, as you will be well aware, your body was conceived out of the interaction of your father's sperm (which had developed for 74 days in his testes) with your mother's ovum (which had been incubating in her body since she herself was a foetus in your grandmother's womb). Following conception, those body fluids developed into a foetus which grew in your mother's womb for about 9 months and then experienced birth.

If you are the new born body ... then by implication you are not only the developing foetus but you must also be the sperm which existed in your father for 2 ½ months and the ovum which existed in your mother since before her own birth. Even though those genetic fluids were a part of your parent's bodies ... you are that genetic material. In other words you are parts of other people's bodies.

As the genetic fluids of your parents, you not only existed prior to birth, you existed prior to conception. If you truly are the body then by implication you existed in the absence of conception.

~

Following birth, when you first experienced your body it was like a foreign object to you. You couldn't control it. You couldn't voluntarily move your limbs, your head rolled around and you had to be cared for by other people. All your actions – such as crying, blinking and sucking – were instinctive reflexes.

Through repeated movements you learned how to use your body. You began to coordinate your movements and became so familiar with your body that it no longer seemed like a foreign object.

However, even though you may now identify with that body, it doesn't make it any less of a foreign object. The majority of its functions still operate independently of your will and conscious awareness. It remains foreign and mysterious to you.

It wouldn't be an exaggeration to say that if you are the body, then by and large you are a foreign and indeed a mysterious object.

~

Even though your body is a collection of atoms which are shaped by genetic factors, the particular body that you now experience is a product of the food that you have eaten. Through the act of digestion that food is transformed into blood, flesh and bone.

The food that is eaten today becomes your body tomorrow. As such, if you are the body then you are the food that you have eaten.

And if you really believe that you are the body then the next time you eat something you could reasonably conclude ... now, I am about to eat myself. Ridiculous isn't it!

⁓

To extend the argument, if you are the body and by implication the food that you have eaten, then you are also the multiplicity of life forms you have consumed ... every plant and every animal. And when you are stung by a mosquito or other insect, the food of your body becomes theirs. As such, if you are your body do you also become part of the mosquito?

The body of one becomes the body of another – so whose body is it?

The ultimate conclusion is that you are either all bodies ... or none.

⁓

And of course the food that you eat is external to you.

When you consume and digest this external product, the nutrients are converted into limbs, organs and systems.

However, even though it has been put to use and its appearance has been modified, in essence it remains an external factor.

If you are the body ... then you are a collection of external factors.

⁓

What's more, your body is constantly changing in appearance and composition each and every day.

New cells are produced and old cells die every moment. The body is in constant change. It is never the same from one moment to the next. Your body now is different from the body you had at the start of this chapter, let alone the body you had 20 years ago and will have in 20 years' time.

If you are the body ... then which particular appearance or composition are you?

⁓

Of course while your body is a unique appearance, in actuality there is nothing individual about it. Your body is a product of its environment; relies on that environment for its survival and can't be separated from that environment.

While that body might appear to be yours, there is no separate body that you can say 'this is mine'.

Whatever body you think is yours is actually an indivisible part of the rest of the universe and doesn't belong to any individual. The appearance of an individual body is an illusion.

If you are the body, just where does your body start and finish? Which body is actually you?

—

Even though you may believe you are the body now, when it no longer serves your purpose you discard it, not only hair, nails and skin, but other significant body parts such as arms, legs and organs if they threaten your survival.

And there will come a day when you discard this body of yours altogether without a second thought, and others will bury or burn it as an as an unwanted dead object.

If you are the body, are you also those discarded parts? Are you that dead object?

—

Doesn't it seem untenable to believe that you are the body? Surely, it makes more sense to understand the body as a useful instrument.

You use that body to sense, perceive and communicate … but 'what you are' is not that biological apparatus.

You use the food you eat, but you are not that food. The act of digestion doesn't create what you are.

No matter how much you identify with the body, it is only a tool ... it is not you.

~

When you consider that whatever aspect of your body you perceive appears as a mental image in your mind, it should not be surprising to realise that you are not the body.

That image appears to you but you are not that image.

~

The belief that you are the body is a major misunderstanding.

If you are to realise self then you need to understand deeply, profoundly and completely that, despite your strong attachments, what you are is not the body. Refuse to consider yourself as such. Stop identifying with it.

You are not the body.

35 You are not the self-image

Another major source of identification is a person's self-image.

The self-image is the ideas that a person has about themself. It consists of impressions about appearance, ability, character or any other trait, whether inherited or learned. These impressions may arise from personal experience or be shaped by the judgments of others.

The self-image is usually an important aspect of anyone's identity. But does that mean that you are the self-image?

In this chapter we will consider whether you could be the self-image.

~

As you go through life a mental picture of your world develops. A significant aspect of this picture is the self-image you form.

This self-image develops as a product of experiences and exists as a collection of non-conscious, sub-conscious and conscious memories. Even though the resulting impression may be remarkably complex and multidimensional, it nevertheless exists as a mental image.

As such, if you are the self-image then you are a picture which appears in your mind. There is nothing tangible about you.

If you are comfortable with the idea that you are a mental image, there is an additional complication.

No self-image remains the same. Not only does it change with major life events (such as becoming a parent) but also with relatively minor fluctuations of mood ("I was pleased with myself, but now I'm disappointed").

If you are the self-image, then it begs the question, which one are you? Are you the self-image you had on a particular day as a child? The self-image you have now? Or the self-image you will have at some point in the future?

If you are one particular self-image, why not another?

You could of course claim that you are not any one self-image, instead you are actually a collection of all the self-images you have ever had.

Putting aside the issue that you would be claiming to be totally different self-images, there is another issue to resolve.

While you have accounted for all your changing self-images, you haven't accounted for that aspect of you which exists when you are unconscious or drift into deep sleep. In that blankness you don't even know you exist, let alone have a self-image about what you are.

If you are the self-image, then what are you when you don't have a self-image?

~

The fact that you alternate between having a self-image and not having a self-image indicates that your reality isn't the self-image ... any or all of them.

You are what you are with a particular self-image, with another self-image and, crucially, without those self-images. I'd suggest that you are what you are without any and all self-images. Any self-image is, after all, just a mental picture which appears to you. It represents a learned aspect of self. You are what you are with that learning but crucially you are what you are without it.

Even if you identify with the information you learn, you aren't that information. That information appears to you, but it is not you. While it may alternatively appear and disappear in your mind, you don't.

~

This principle doesn't just apply to relatively insignificant aspects of the self-image, such as the colour of hair or IQ score. Nor does it just apply to more significant aspects such as the achievements of a lifetime. It applies to even the most fundamental aspects of the self-image.

If you believe that in essence you are a soul, a spirit, an ethereal body, realise that this is just another aspect of the self-image. It might be an interesting aspect. It might be very important to you. You might even build your life upon that belief. Nevertheless, it is still just a self-image.

As a self-image, regardless of how subtle, profound or otherworldly it may be, and regardless of how convinced you may be that it represents your truth, it is just a mental image.

You aren't that mental image you have about yourself or any other.

No mental image can approach the reality of what you are.

—

In any case, any self-image is more a reflection of the conditioning forces inherent in your environment than it is of you. A simple change in the environment can dramatically alter the self-image.

Inasmuch as the environment is external to what you are, so too is any self-image learned from that environment. As such, it could be argued that any image which results from that environment belongs to that environment. It isn't even your own, let alone you.

⁓

I would like to suggest that the self-image is only ever a picture of who you are ... not what you are.

The self-image appears to you but it is not what you are. Actually, the self-image is what you are not.

Identification with any self-image is not only a limitation of what you are, but an obstacle to self-realisation.

36 You are not a separate entity

Even though you may be prepared to concede that you aren't the body and can appreciate the logic that you aren't a mental image, I'm sure that you will still harbour the notion that you are a separate entity of some description. That entity may be a soul, spirit or energy, but regardless of the particular description, it will be some essence which you consider is uniquely and individually you.

In this chapter I want to challenge that belief simply because there is no such thing as a separate entity.

~

If I were to describe the formation of the earth as a storm of interacting stardust, I guess that I could be accused of over-simplification, but for our purposes it will suffice.

Conceptually speaking, some 5 billion or so years ago, earth was a seething mass of stardust which happened to settle at a particular distance from the newly developed sun, happened to ensnare its own satellite (the moon) and happened to have a 23 degree axis tilt ... all of which were conducive to the development of life.

As the planet cooled and coalesced, complex reactions occurred amongst the stardust ... water appeared and an atmosphere developed. Further interaction resulted in the emergence of a plethora of life forms, ultimately appearing as a diverse multitude, each with its unique qualities and characteristics.

These life forms may seem to possess their own individual bodies, but in essence they are that ancient stardust. While they appear to emerge from the mix as separate entities, they are actually an intrinsic part of that mix and can't be separated from it. Despite appearances to the contrary, they are that stardust.

~

The life forms not only emerge from that stardust environment, but continue to depend on that evolving stardust environment for air, food, light and water. Without it, the life forms can't survive or exist.

I would suggest that this is not indicative of a close relationship between life form and environment, but the fact that there is absolutely no separation between them. What emerges from the environment and continues to depend on it isn't separate to the environment; it is an inseparable expression of that environment. It is the environment.

There are no separate entities. They don't emerge from the environment, exist in the environment, or are separate from the environment. All is just environment.

~

The appearance of what may seem to be individual or separate is an illusion. When examined, that appearance is revealed as a product of a network of relationships which extend across the universe.

It neither exists separately nor independently from the whole. In fact, it is the whole merely appearing as an individual and separate part.

Any notion that any aspect of the whole can exist separately or independently is entirely a figment of the mind.

⌢

If we continue with this line of thought we can make the point that every physical, mental, energetic and spiritual aspect of the person you think you are is derived from the world around you ... and depends on that world for its continuation.

All the aspects which you think are 'you' are actually expressions of the environment. There is no individual aspect which you can say 'this is me'. There is no separate 'you'.

Any idea that there is a 'you' separate to the environment is erroneous. You are so much a part of your environment that 'you' are indistinguishable from it.

You are not in any way separate from the flow of life. You are not going along with that flow. You are not even an intrinsic part of that flow. In fact, you are that flow.

~

The implication is that even though people may assume that they are a separate entity living a life and pursuing their own ends, it is not so. There is no such separate entity.

And while people may believe that there must be something which is quintessentially them – an executive 'I' which is in charge scanning senses, assessing experiences and making decisions – it isn't true. The 'I' is just another aspect of the illusion of separateness.

While the separate 'I' seems to be an undeniably real aspect of self, it is actually inferred from experiences. Despite the most intensive search, that 'I' cannot be discovered anywhere in the brain, mind or universe.

Why? Well, I would suggest because it does not exist.

Nothing is separate from the environment – not the body, not the mind and, definitely, not the vague persuasion 'I'.

~

In an indivisible world there are no individual or separate entities.

There is life ... but not an independent entity 'I' that lives a life. There is perceiving ... but not a separate 'I' which does the perceiving. There is experiencing ... but not a discrete 'I' which has the experiences. There is thinking ... but not an objective 'I' which has thoughts. There is feeling ... but not an isolated 'I' which feels. There is understanding ... but not an individual 'I' which understands.

Living, perceiving, experiencing, observing, thinking and feeling happens ... but not to an individual separate entity.

The belief that there is such an entity is pure imagination. It is a fundamental misunderstanding.

⁓

Undoubtedly, this is a confronting topic and it wouldn't be surprising if you cling to the idea that you must be a separate or individual something. I certainly did ... but it is a grave error to think this way.

If you insist on believing that you are a separate entity, my challenge to you is to discover that aspect of you which exists separately and independently from everything else.

In my experience it can't be discovered.

Why? Because it doesn't exist. Everything is, in fact, whole. All is indivisibly one.

⁓

Rather than an individual entity, I would suggest that it may be helpful to consider yourself more like a rainbow!

Let me explain …

A rainbow arises as the result of a particular mix of conditions … namely sun shining on water vapour. While those conditions are present, the rainbow appears. When those conditions cease, the rainbow disappears.

Despite the appearance of the rainbow, it never existed as an entity: there was no core to it. It was only ever a product of conditions.

When the rainbow appears it doesn't come from anywhere and when it disappears it doesn't go anywhere. It simply appears when the right conditions emerge and disappears when those conditions no longer exist.

Without the right conditions, the 'rainbow' exists as water vapour and sunlight … and not as a rainbow.

～

Similarly, you the person only appear as a product of the right mix of conditions.

The body is formed out of the particular convergence of egg and sperm. It is sustained by food and develops bones, flesh, blood, conscious awareness and experiences. And, as a result of those conditions, forms the idea that it is a separate entity, somehow separate from its environment.

Every aspect of its existence – body, brain, mind and consciousness – is a product of various conditions. When the conditions are right, the person appears and lives its allotted span. And just like the rainbow, when those conditions no longer exist, the person disappears. It doesn't go anywhere. It just ceases to appear once the conditions which converged to support it cease.

At no time is a separate entity involved. Instead, like an onion, the person is all layers but no core: all appearance but no substance.

⁓

The idea of a separate entity … an executive 'I' … a real 'me' … is a mistaken inference. It only seems plausible because it is accepted without question and never investigated.

Question the existence of that separate entity – get to the bottom of it – and it will dissolve like the figment it is.

⁓

The idea 'I am a separate entity' of whatever description is nothing but a misunderstanding. Clinging to that mistake will block self-realisation.

To realise what you are … you must cease believing what you cannot be.

Relinquish the notion that you are a separate entity.

Separate entities do not exist.

37 You are not what you observe

Just as an eye can see all that passes its field of vision but not itself, so you perceive all around you but not what you are.

While you look for yourself within the field of what you perceive, sense or experience, the reality of what you are will remain obscured.

Regardless of what you observe, you aren't that. To the contrary, you are that which observes.

The sooner you realise that you aren't anything you perceive … the sooner you will come to the startling realisation of what you are.

～

Your world is comprised of countless observable objects. They may appear to be 'physical' such as chairs and tables, or 'mental' such as thoughts, feelings and sensations. However, while you observe those objects – whether a physical chair or a mental sensation – you are always the subject.

As subject, 'you' can never be observed as an object. In fact, you can't be observed. As soon as you try to observe any aspect of 'you', it immediately becomes another object under observation and therefore not you, the subject.

Many objects appear to you, but as subject, you don't exist as an object and can't be discovered as one.

You are the complete absence of objects.

~

The principle that you aren't what you observe is simple. Take the following example.

If you observe a rock then you know that you can't be that rock, as you are that which observes the rock. Similarly, if you observe your arm then you know that you can't be that arm. Or if you observe your entire body then you know that you aren't that body. Likewise, if you observe a thought or feeling, or, indeed, all your thoughts and feelings then you know that you can't be any of those experiences. And if you can observe your consciousness then you know that you aren't that either.

Actually, regardless of what you sense, perceive or experience, the fact that you sense, perceive or experience it demonstrates that you aren't that. You are always that which senses, perceives or experiences but not what you sense, perceive or experience.

As such, anything physical, mental, emotional or spiritual you observe ... you know that you can't be that.

Rather, they are objects which appear to you, the subject.

As subject, you observe them and so you can't be them. As subject you can't be observed.

~

The ramifications of this simple principle are startlingly profound. Inasmuch as the mind can understand in terms of objects, try as it might, it can't grasp the subject of those objects.

The result is that while the mind can comprehend all that you aren't, it cannot have positive knowledge about what you are. It can't comprehend you as the subject.

As subject, what you are is altogether beyond the intellectual, emotional or artistic capacity of the mind.

What you are doesn't appear as a conceivable object in your mind because your reality isn't a conceivable object. Actually, it is the other way around; your mind is a conceivable object which appears to the reality of what you are.

~

One analogy which may help to illustrate the point of this chapter is that of the purest space in a red glass container. For the purpose of the analogy, the space is aware.

To the space everything around it looks red and so it infers that it is red as well. It can also make out the shape of the glass container and so it presumes that it has the shape of the container.

However, despite these impressions, the space is neither the colour red nor the shape of the container.

The colour and shape may provide a reference point, but while its self-analysis is in terms of colour and shape, it can't know what it is. Colour and shape indicate *that* it is, but don't reveal *what* it isn't.

That purest space is forever beyond the limitations of the redness and the form of the container.

~

Similarly, if you only know yourself in terms of what is perceived, conceived or observed, then you don't know self.

If your self-awareness is restricted to the mental objects which cross the screen of your mind, there can be no self-knowledge.

Self-realisation can only dawn when you cease reliance on the conceptual and start to move beyond the mental picture.

~

To realise what you are, first discover all that you aren't: body, mind, senses, beliefs. Only then can your spaceless nature dawn on you.

Realise that whatever you observe points to the fact of your reality, but that regardless of what is observed you are not that. While what you observe does not reveal what you are, it serves the purpose of reminding you what you aren't.

It's not even wise to consider yourself as spaceless, as that too is just another observable mental image and therefore not what you are.

⌐

Just as a person with a torch can observe all in front of them and know that what they observe isn't them, so too you can be aware that you are not anything which crosses your field of attention.

While your identity is based on experiences, memories and ideas … you cannot but help to remain ignorant of what you are.

⌐

On the journey of self-realisation, any assertion about what you are demands denial.

Holding onto anything is an obstacle and just part of the problem.

⌐

Undoubtedly, the full and complete knowledge of what you *aren't* is attainable.

That revelation will lead you to the startling realisation of what you are.

38 You are not the person

Conventional wisdom will tell you that you are a real person living in a real world; that you are a thing among things, existing in time and space; and that you are born and will die.

This may seem to be such an obvious statement that you never think to question it. Even if it was suggested that the claim that you are a person is actually an assumption, you may grudgingly acknowledge the point, but note that it is an unassailable assumption. And if it were asserted that this unassailable assumption was in fact mistaken, it wouldn't be surprising if you still vigorously resisted any such suggestion that you are not a person.

This is understandable. The idea that you are a person seems to be so obvious that it is beyond reproach. After all, how could you be anything other than the person you have always taken yourself to be.

I would, however, like to suggest that the assumption that you are a person is very much like the assumption of the villagers in chapter 1 who firmly believed that the sun moved across the sky. While it may seem self-evident, it is actually a misunderstanding.

If you consider the points that have been raised over the last few chapters, I would suggest that the conclusion that you are not a person is inescapable.

- You are not the body. The body is comprised of ancient atoms. It is shaped by the genetic material of other people. And it is a collection of the food you have eaten. This constantly changing mass is not so much 'you' as an instrument you use.

- You are not the self-image. The self-image is a mental image. It is a non-tangible phenomenon which exists in mind. This mental image not only constantly changes, it disappears altogether. The self-image is a picture which appears to you, but you are not that picture.

- You are not a separate entity. Everything is intrinsic to and inseparable from its environment. Nothing is separate from anything else. You are not an individual or separate anything.

- You are not anything you observe. Whatever you observe is an object. You cannot observe the subject which is observing. Whatever you observe, you are not that.

If you aren't a body, self-image, separate entity or anything observable, you can't be the person you think you are either.

⌣

The idea that you aren't a person will seem very strange if you've always considered yourself as one. However, the key to understanding this perspective goes back to our discussions in the first part of the book.

If you recall, it was suggested that, while your world may appear to be a tangible reality, it actually exists as an appearance in your mind.

If we extend this point, then it isn't too difficult to appreciate that everything about 'you' the person – whether physiological or biological, intellectual or emotional, energetic or spiritual – can similarly be understood as a mental image appearing in the mind.

Even though the person may appear to be a tangible reality, may be endowed with special qualities and capabilities, and may have achieved many remarkable feats, all can still be appreciated as a mental picture.

There's nothing about the person you think you are – whether sensation, experience, memory, appearance, thought or feeling – that cannot be perceived as a mental image.

⁓

Having appreciated that your world is a mental phenomenon, the person you have taken yourself to be can similarly be perceived as part of that mental picture. It may be an integral part, but nevertheless it is no more tangible than the rest of your world in which it appears.

Even though you may be deeply attached to that changing image, I would suggest that the person you take yourself to be is no more real than anything else in your world.

Just as the world is an image in your mind, so too is the person which appears in that world. World and person in that world are part and parcel of the one mental picture.

⁓

While you can observe these different aspects of the person which appear in your mind, the fact that you observe them tells you that you are not them.

The mental image of the person appears as an object but you aren't that object. There is a deeper aspect to you which lies beyond that mental picture.

What you are can't be found as a mental image appearing in your mind. Indeed, those mental images appear to you, you never appear as one or even all of them.

Crucially you are what you are while there is a mental image but also when there are none. You are the support for all changing appearances of the person.

⁓

The analogy of a dream that we used in the first part of the book may help to explain the point.

If you recall we noted that when you dream you experience a dreamed world which can seem very real. It can be populated which seemingly real landscapes, buildings and streets, yet it is a dream.

Similarly, in that dreamed world you inevitably dream about the central character of the dream – 'you' – a seemingly real person who finds themselves in a range of seemingly real situations and has seemingly real experiences. While this 'you' appears to be real, tangible and genuinely have a life of its own, it is neither real nor tangible, and has no independent life. Everything about this version of 'you' exists as a dreamed figure.

This dreamed figure may represent you and you may strongly identify with it – wishing it success and fearing for its safety – but despite your attachment you aren't that dreamed figure. As the dreamer, you are actually beyond the dream and can't be discovered in it.

While you are dreaming you may find it impossible to believe that you could be anything other than the dreamed figure, but when you wake it becomes obvious that the figure, along with the rest of your dreamed world, was only a dream which appeared in your mind.

~

I would suggest that this situation is very similar to your relationship with the person you think you are.

The image of a seemingly real person appears in your mind, much like a dream. But your reality is beyond the mental image of the person. You aren't a mental image and can't be discovered as one.

Your mental world isn't observed by 'you' a real person who experiences that world, instead both world and person are mental images which appear to 'you'. That 'you' is the reality which neither appears nor exists as a mental image.

For now you don't need to try and understand what you are, just realise that you are not the mental image of the person, regardless of how real it might seem or how attached to it you are.

~

To observe the person, identify with the person and believe that you are that person, is a great misunderstanding.

That person is a mental object. It is a picture which appears to you. You can observe, explore and even enjoy that person, but it is not your reality.

You are *not* the person.

~

The stubborn belief that you are the person is an insurmountable obstacle to self-realisation.

To realise what you are, refuse to believe that you are the person. Distance yourself. Observe the person's patterned behaviours. Observe what it senses and how it reacts. Observe its thoughts and feelings. Observe its desires and fears. Recognise them as conditioned forms of behaviour ... mere appearances in mind. Appreciate the entirety of the person as the mental image that it is. And know that you are not that.

In the absence of all false identification, your indescribable reality will dawn on you.

With rationality and sincerity of desire it is inevitable.

39 The journey is your own

Having considered what you aren't – body, self-image, separate entity, observable object, person – the next step on our journey is to consider other obstacles which may prevent the realisation of what you are.

As these obstacles are more personal in nature than the intellectual obstacles that have been considered to date, it is a timely juncture to briefly consider the nature of the journey that lies ahead and the key ingredient which is crucial to the success of your journey.

~

Self-realisation is different to all other understanding because, unlike all other understanding, the reality of what you are can't be conceptualised as a mental image. Indeed, whatever concept you form about your reality, you are not that.

As such, although your reality is undeniable, it is beyond words. What you are can't be squeezed into any verbal formulation. No self-definition is valid.

Words and concepts can't capture what you are any more than they can capture the taste of sugar or the smell of a rose. If you only know words and concepts, then not only do you not know the taste of sugar or the smell of a rose, you certainly don't know the profundity of the self.

～

The implication is that no belief, philosophy or ideology can teach you what you are. Self-realisation can never be a mere conversion to a different set of ideas, beliefs or philosophies. In fact, accumulated head knowledge only serves as a further obstacle to overcome.

This is not to say that words are of no use. To the contrary, words may be very useful.

They can certainly draw attention to the fact that self-realisation is possible and can indicate the benefits which flow from it. They can also be useful in identifying obstacles which may prevent self-realisation and can even articulate a suggested course of action as to how self may be realised.

Words, though, can't enlighten.

If they are relied on, they can frustrate real understanding, and prove to be more hindrance than help.

～

While it is true that self-realisation results in fresh and inspiring ideas, heightened levels of experience, and profound ways of seeing the world; the way to self-realisation isn't through descriptions about those results.

Instead, it is necessary to go beyond all reliance on words and ideas ... and cross from the verbal to the non-verbal, from the conceptual to the non-conceptual, from ideas to direct experience.

This isn't achieved by merely reading or considering the words, but rather by the action which is taken on them. If the words remain as just ideas, they are pointless. They must be put into practice. Only what you discover through our own experience will be of any real use. That deeper sense of knowing is imperative.

‑

Self-realisation can only come through your own investigations. No one else can do it for you. Words can point the way but the journey depends on you.

The action you take is critical.

You have to realise what you are directly for yourself. It must be your experience. There is no substitute.

‑

Undoubtedly, the crucial element in the journey of self-realisation is desire. A person must really want to know what they are.

Without desire a person will be content with their conceptual understanding – I am a person, I am a human being, I am a spirit, I am a soul, I am an astral being –

and won't have any interest in realising what they are beyond those concepts. No amount of encouragement will shake them out of this inertia. Self-realisation will elude them.

Even a genuine interest isn't sufficient if it only amounts to an intellectual exercise. Without the desire to understand in more than a thinking sense, there will be a disconnect between ideas and action. A conceptual understanding will be realised but self will remain a mystery.

Deep desire is what is necessary. With it the person will not only be fascinated by the promise of self-knowledge, but will find it becomes the top priority in their life. Armed with the courage to admit and confront their ignorance they will overcome all obstacles. The direct experience of self is achievable for them.

⁓

While words can guide, the journey is up to you. Desire is the key.

The question is: do you really want to know what you are?

If so, then you will naturally give your heart and mind to self-discovery. No obstacles will be too great for you to overcome.

40 The opportunity of unhappiness

The point has been made that you already are what you are. There is nothing that you can do to change what you are, nor is there anything that you can do to learn what you are.

As such, the path to self-realisation is not a process of gathering fresh information about your reality but, instead, removing the obstacles which prevent you from realising what you are.

So far we've identified all that, logically, you cannot be. You cannot be the body, the self-image, a separate entity, anything you observe or even the person you have always taken yourself to be. These are certainly significant insights on the path to self-realisation; however these insights only take us so far ... they only tell you what you are not. Even if you are convinced by these arguments and accept that you are not any of these phenomena, you still have no positive understanding as to what you are.

Sure, you may be able to form fresh ideas about the nature of your reality (you are not the body, not the self-image, not a separate entity, not anything that can be observed and not the person), but those vague ideas are not self-realisation. If you hold onto them they will obscure your reality.

To realise what you are without recourse to any ideas, all obstacles must be removed.

~

As we've noted, deep desire is a pre-requisite for self-realisation, for without it there won't be the necessary motivation to recognise the obstacles which prevent self-realisation, let alone relinquish them.

This is certainly the case with regard to the first set of obstacles we've addressed that define 'what you are' in terms of what you cannot be (the body, the self-image, and so on). It is especially the case with the next class of obstacles, which concern mistaken assumptions about 'me' and 'mine'. While, this second set of obstacles are, just like the first, assumptions, there are some notable differences.

First, they are harder to identify. They are usually buried deep in the psyche and may not be readily recognisable. In fact, owing to years of implicit acceptance, even if they are identified, they may not be seen as problematic.

Second, they almost inevitably comprise a significant emotional component.

Third, they are highly idiosyncratic. The particular assumption varies from person to person. As such, it is incumbent on the 'person' to identify them for themselves.

Over the next few chapters our focus will be on identifying (as much as possible) these personal obstacles. The logical point of entry will be to consider unhappiness, not only as a tool to identify these obstacles but also as opportunity to progress your spiritual journey.

～

I think that the first point to note is that while we may not be aware of the obstacle, we may, nevertheless, be aware of the result that it produces. That result is experienced as unhappiness.

Because of the existence of unhappiness we can be aware that there is an imbalance or disharmony, which can then be traced to an underlying mistaken assumption. That mistaken assumption is the obstacle. It not only results in unhappiness, it serves as an impediment to self-realisation.

Certainly, without that false assumption, disharmony isn't created, unhappiness doesn't arise and there is one less obstacle to self-realisation. Accordingly, unhappiness is not only a prime indicator of the existence of mistaken assumptions; it also represents a guiding light on the path to self-realisation.

The unhappiness you experience on a day to day basis indicates the obstacles you need to identify and the journey of relinquishment you need to take. As you explore the mistaken assumptions that create unhappiness, you are inexorably drawn closer to the realisation of your reality.

~

Of course, unhappiness is a common experience. While it can be described as a sensation that something is missing, lacking, not quite right or perhaps very wrong, it is not limited to a particular feeling. Instead it varies greatly in expression.

It can be experienced as sadness, disappointment, loneliness or anxiety, but also annoyance, frustration or anger, and even hatred. It can be fleeting or enduring. It may absorb all of a person's attention or they may be barely aware of it.

Crucially though, unhappiness is a personal experience. No two people experience the same unhappiness let alone the same combination of unhappiness.

As such, the lessons that can be learned from unhappiness are peculiar to each person. It is up to the person to learn the lessons which are relevant to them.

While this book can't tell you what lessons you have to learn, it can offer some thoughts about how to approach unhappiness.

~

In this regard, we can note that while there may be a temptation to blame unhappiness on 'external' factors, such as misfortune or the wilful action of others, it is not externally imposed.

Unhappiness is actually a product of reactions and thinking processes. As a product of the particular mindset, the person creates and perpetuates their unhappiness ... even if in ignorance.

That said, it is true that the particular combination of reactions and thinking processes do result from formative conditioning forces resulting in learned habits. Even so, unhappiness is not beyond a person's control.

If a person wants to be free of unhappiness or, for that matter, attain self-realisation, it is eminently possible, but they must take responsibility for their unhappiness and learn the lessons that unhappiness has to teach them.

Unhappiness offers a valuable opportunity.

~

As there may be some resistance to the notion that unhappiness is not externally imposed, I'd like to offer a simple example, from which we can extrapolate some general principles. Consider the situation where photos are burned in a fire.

If I am upset by the loss of these photos it may be quite tempting to blame my unhappiness on the fact of the fire (an external event beyond my control). However, it is also true that another person may be quite unperturbed by the loss of the photos and not give them a second thought.

Why is it that we can have such different reactions?

If it were true that unhappiness was due to the fact of the fire we could expect that both of us would be unhappy. However, as this isn't the case, the unhappiness I experience can't just be attributed to the external event of the fire. There must be another factor at play which generates unhappiness in me but indifference in the other person.

I would suggest that rather than the external event, the decisive factor is the respective attitude to the photos.

As such, the reason I felt unhappy was because the photos had particular sentimental significance to me and I didn't want to lose them, while the other person didn't feel unhappy because they didn't have an interest in old photos and weren't attached to them.

The fact that the same situation results in distress to me but indifference to another is indicative that unhappiness isn't inherent in the situation but, rather, the attitude.

What makes a situation good, bad or indifferent is the attitude. It is the attitude which determines unhappiness, not the situation. The 'pure' situation is neither good nor bad nor indifferent … nor author of unhappiness.

～

While this example may be rather trite, it encapsulates a principle which is applicable to all unhappiness. Unhappiness isn't so much determined by what happens, but by the attitudes-ideas-beliefs-desires-expectations about what should happen.

Of course, the situation does have a role to play, maybe even a significant role. However, the situation is not the source of unhappiness. Rather, the situation merely triggers the underlying propensity for unhappiness, which already exists as patterns of thinking, feeling and reacting in the mind of the person.

As such, unhappiness isn't inherent in the situation. Instead it is an emotional reaction to the situation. It is what the person adds. It is how the person has been conditioned to respond.

It's not 'the world' which is the problem … but your mind. State of mind is what makes the state of your world. State of mind is state of world.

—

We could also note that while the attitude-idea-belief-desire-expectation is a significant aspect of unhappiness, an even more crucial element is the attachment to that mindset.

It is that attachment to what should or shouldn't happen which provokes a person to resist situations which challenge their mindset. The result is that as the person resists the situation, the feeling of unhappiness is generated. Resistance is the feeling of unhappiness.

The more a person resists their situation, the more unhappiness they experience.

Situations don't create unhappiness, resistance to them does. Attachment and resistance are the lifeblood of unhappiness. Without attachment there is no resistance or unhappiness.

⁓

If we enquire as to why the attachment arises in the first place we can usually identify an underlying assumption about 'me' and 'mine' – about what I am and what I need.

If the assumption is false, then unhappiness is inevitable; but if there is no false assumption unhappiness can't arise.

By becoming aware of false assumptions, unhappiness can be dissolved and otherwise hidden obstacles to self-realisation can be overcome.

⁓

Resistance to any situation is the problem. If you don't want to be so unhappy don't resist so much. If you don't want to be unhappy at all, don't resist at all.

By changing your reaction, you change the situation.

Once you are free from all resistance you are master of any situation.

~

To be free of unhappiness, be free of resistance. To be free of resistance, be free of false assumptions.

Make your mind right and all will be right.

41 Approaching unhappiness

As a person goes about their daily life, they encounter situations which challenge their mistaken views of self. Out of self-love they try to preserve and protect that ego. They resist those situations and unhappiness arises. The more they cling to their mistaken view of self, the more unhappiness they experience.

The unhappiness isn't a pleasant experience and so the person tries to avoid, supress or escape it by seeking more pleasurable experiences. This reaction is understandable, but the consequences are fourfold.

- While the unhappiness may be temporarily avoided, it is not eradicated. As such, the same unhappiness will resurface even when different people and situations are involved. By avoiding the unhappiness it is actually perpetuated.

- This habit of avoiding unhappiness, results in the mistaken perception that unhappiness is an entirely negative experience. As such, the opportunity it presents for positive growth is not appreciated.

- The reluctance to learn from unhappiness, results in a tendency to accept it as an inevitable fact of life, which prevents its resolution.

- And by not effectively dealing with the unhappiness, it tends to get worse. The corollary is that the attempts to escape it become more extreme.

In this chapter we will consider positive approaches to dealing with unhappiness.

—

The fact that a person experiences unhappiness is evidence that there is a lesson to learn. It is an indication that a person's approach has not met the challenges presented by the situation.

I would go further and say that the person's approach not only determines their experience of the situation but also the nature of the challenges inherent in it. Both the experience and the associated challenge are measures of the quality of the approach. A change in the approach, changes the experience, the challenge and, by implication, the situation.

If the approach is appropriate, unhappiness will not arise. However, if the approach is in any way problematic then varying degrees of unhappiness are inevitable.

To be free of unhappiness it's imperative to adopt an approach unaligned with false assumptions.

—

While the appropriate approach may not be readily apparent, it can be discovered by learning from the unhappiness generated by inappropriate approaches.

As such, unhappiness is not an experience to be avoided or supressed; rather, it is an experience to be appreciated and learned from. It represents a significant opportunity for personal enrichment.

Unhappiness is the message that there are issues which need to be addressed. But more than a message, it is a guide. It illuminates obstacles which would otherwise remain hidden. It reveals the path to self-realisation.

Unhappiness represents a wonderful opportunity. It is a terrific blessing ... but only if the person learns from it.

~

Of course, there are just as many ways to learn from unhappiness as there are lessons to be learnt. No one approach is necessarily better than another. The decisive factor is what works for you.

How do you know if your approach is working? The answer must be by the results it achieves. If the unhappiness doesn't arise again, then you know that your approach is working.

I would like to share with you the approach I adopted. I am not saying that it is the only approach nor even the best, but it did work for me.

Think of my suggestions as a general guide which you can adapt to suit your needs.

~

The first step is to recognise that you feel unhappy. It may be a trifling annoyance or a more significant frustration, but what is important is that you are able to admit that you feel unhappy.

That might seem obvious – which it is – but it can be surprisingly difficult. Even if you feel unhappy it can be challenging to admit it to yourself, let alone other people. It is far easier to convince yourself that there is no problem and that no action needs to be taken, rather than open yourself to the fresh pain which comes from admitting that you are unhappy.

However, this acknowledgement is vital. While unhappiness is in any way denied, dismissed or made light of, its lessons can't be learned.

The unhappiness must be acknowledged and owned.

There is no other way. You can't learn from what you don't acknowledge.

~

Having recognised the unhappiness, the next step is to take responsibility for it.

As unhappiness isn't an enjoyable sensation, there is a natural tendency to alleviate its effects through denial or diversion. However, while this may make the unhappiness more tolerable, it is not taking the necessary responsibility.

In order to take responsibility for unhappiness you can't avoid it, instead you must turn and face it. Rather than shirk its unpleasantness, embrace the unhappiness so that you can gain deep insights into its causes and effects.

This doesn't mean that you need to get caught up in the unhappiness and feel miserable, but rather that you approach it critically with a view to learning from it.

If you don't take responsibility for your unhappiness nobody else can or will.

—

So the first two steps of the approach are to admit that you are unhappy and then to take responsibility for it. The next step is to put these principles into practice.

You can work with whatever unhappiness you choose, however, at first it may be easier to work with relatively minor unhappiness that may be bugging you. This is only a guide though, not a rule. It's up to you.

You also have the option of working with the unhappiness as it arises in real time, though it may be easier to reflect upon it once the heat of the moment has passed. Again, it's a matter for you.

~

As you've acknowledged that you feel unhappy and are prepared to take responsibility for it, the next thing to do is describe the relevant facts which gave rise to your unhappiness.

For example, you could say, "I was doing this but then that happened". "I wanted to do this but that prevented me from doing it." "I was feeling good but then this person said that to me."

The key is to articulate the cold relevant facts. Don't judge or blame, just state what happened or didn't happen.

~

Once you have outlined the situation then turn your attention to the unhappiness you feel.

Let yourself feel the sensation of unhappiness you experience. Observe what it feels like to be unhappy. Notice the sensations in your body: how your head and chest feel. Become aware of your rate of breathing. Notice the thoughts in your mind: see how they race.

Then try to articulate the unhappiness you feel. For example, "I feel agitated, upset, sad, disappointed, frustrated, angry, lonely, bored". Try to be as accurate as you can with your description. Try to arrive at a description which captures your feeling.

It may well be the case that the unhappiness you experience is comprised of many different aspects ... for example, a combination of fear, anger and sadness.

The important thing is to become as consciously aware of your experience of unhappiness and its different aspects as possible.

—

The next step is to then observe how you want to deal with your unhappiness. How do you want to react?

Do you feel like eating food or drinking alcohol? Do you want to light up a cigarette? Do you want to go for a run? Do you want to be with people or do you want to be alone? Do you want to scream? Do you want to take revenge?

Whatever you want to do isn't as important as becoming aware of your impulse reaction. Don't act on that impulse, just observe it. Be consciously aware of how you want to deal with the unhappiness.

—

Once you have observed how you feel and how you want to react, then you are ready to dig a bit deeper and understand why you have this feeling of unhappiness.

It will be tempting to blame your unhappiness on what has or hasn't happened, but instead, bring your attention to your own thought processes. What ideas-beliefs-desires-expectations do you have which have triggered your reaction?

Rather than say, "I am unhappy because this or that happened" ... say, "I am unhappy because I wanted this or didn't want that to happen".

Rather than say, "I am unhappy because I am not being respected" ... say, "I am unhappy because I believe that I should be respected".

Rather than say, "I am unhappy because I have been let down" ... say, "I am unhappy because I had an expectation that I shouldn't be let down".

Try to identify your contribution to your unhappiness. Articulate your underlying expectations about what should or should not happen. When the unhappiness isn't very strong it should be fairly easy to uncover. However, if the unhappiness arises from long standing belief patterns from childhood, it may be more challenging to articulate.

⁓

If you can uncover the relevant idea-belief-desire-expectation you will then have a glimpse into the source of your unhappiness.

The existence of that idea-belief-desire-expectation creates the space within which unhappiness can form. You are presented with a set of circumstances which don't conform to your expectations; you resist the unwelcome turn of events and in the process generate unhappiness.

By implication, it should be clear that if you didn't have the particular idea-belief-desire-expectation that you wouldn't resist the situation because there wouldn't be anything to resist and the unhappiness you are now feeling couldn't arise.

You should then be able to conclude ... "I currently feel like this because of this particular belief, however, if I didn't have it then I wouldn't feel like this".

~

Once you reach this level of understanding you then have an interesting choice.

You know that your belief is generating your unhappiness, so the question is, will you decide to maintain the belief and suffer the consequences, or will you let the belief go and be free of the unhappiness.

It actually boils down to a choice between being right and being at peace. You can choose to be right and keep your belief, or you can choose to be at peace and let the belief go.

This is entirely your choice to make. No one can force you to make a decision one way or the other. It is up to you. However, speaking for myself, I go for peace every time.

⌒

I am not suggesting that you shouldn't have ideas-beliefs-desires-expectations. Rather, I am suggesting that you reconsider how firmly you cling to them and how much you are prepared to suffer for them.

If your beliefs and expectations make you feel unhappy, then recognise that they are the problem and, at least, consider relinquishing them. Are they worth the price of unhappiness? Do you want to be the author of your own unhappiness?

Regardless of your decision, having come to this realisation, it should be clear that you don't have to be unhappy. Unhappiness is a choice that you make.

⌒

When the unhappiness is sufficiently strong and the connection to your beliefs and expectations are clear, you will find that you will be willing to abandon even the strongest attachments.

However, why wait till the unhappiness gets this bad. Rather than hold on to beliefs and resist what happens, observe, understand the totality of the situation and respond with wisdom.

If your response is appropriate you won't experience unhappiness. However, if it's not appropriate, you undoubtedly will.

The practice of non-attachment and non-resistance is the practice of spiritual enlightenment.

~

I invite you to see unhappiness as your teacher.

Let it show you the lessons you have to learn. Recognise the problematic ideas-beliefs-desires-expectations that are identified. Appreciate that they are spiritual obstacles to overcome.

Unhappiness shows you how you can grow and develop.

Through attention to unhappiness the worst experiences can be transformed into the best lessons.

By learning from unhappiness you can be free of it ... completely, wholly and permanently.

Stubborn refusal to learn from unhappiness is an insurmountable obstacle to self-realisation.

42 Don't be indifferent

In my experience, once the attachment to the idea-belief-desire-expectation is clearly identified as the cause of unhappiness, the attachment will naturally drop away and the associated unhappiness will dissolve.

If a person is to experience this dissolution they must have a very strong determination to be free of unhappiness.

Without that strong desire, they will not learn from the unhappiness nor make the fundamental shift in thinking and behaviour which is necessary. Instead they will resist the notion that unhappiness is their responsibility, deny that their idea-belief-desire-expectation is the cause of the unhappiness, and refuse to abandon their problematic thought patterns.

The consequence of this unwillingness is that every situation is potentially a means of suffering: even a person's greatest pleasure can be transformed into their greatest sorrow. Unhappiness will remain an inevitable part of life and the obstacles to self-realisation must remain firmly in place.

To be free of unhappiness the person must want this freedom more than anything else. If not, they won't break free of their longstanding habits.

In this chapter I would like to discuss some attitudes which can stymie the necessary determination.

~

First, if the person is in any way attracted to their unhappiness, then they will not have the necessary desire to be free from it.

While it may seem a little strange that someone may be attracted to their unhappiness, it is more common than you may think.

People can be attracted to unhappiness because they get some sort of payoff or reward from being unhappy – whether through the sympathy and attention they receive from others, or the enjoyment of having something to complain about – in which case they will consider (subconsciously at least) their unhappiness to be an asset. As a result they will value their unhappiness or wear it like a badge of honour, and will not be motivated to relinquish it.

If there is any sort of attraction to unhappiness, there won't be sufficient desire to be free from it.

Be aware of attraction to unhappiness.

~

Another reason why a person may not be motivated to be free of unhappiness is because they are expecting some type of vindication for the unhappiness they have experienced.

If they feel that they've had a raw deal in life and expect that these wrongs must be righted, then they won't be prepared to relinquish their unhappiness until they receive the justice they think they deserve. They will expect compensation and want someone to pay for the unhappiness they have so unjustly suffered.

However, what must be understood at the deepest level is that the goal is not justification, compensation or vindication ... but to be free of unhappiness.

Expect nothing from having been unhappy. Have no vested interest.

~

If a person thinks that someone, something or some event can free them from unhappiness, they won't take the necessary responsibility and will remain bound to their unhappiness.

Only the person can eradicate the causes of unhappiness in their life. Things and other people can't do it for them. It is up to the person, and the person alone, to take responsibility for their unhappiness.

Be self-sufficient.

~

It may also be the case that, at heart, the person has very fixed beliefs about what should or shouldn't happen and are not prepared to re-examine or relinquish those beliefs.

If the person is not prepared to reconsider their mindset, even when it is demonstrated to be mistaken or known to cause unhappiness, then the unhappiness must remain.

To be free of unhappiness, it is necessary to be willing to question and relinquish longstanding beliefs.

Be open-minded.

~

Ultimately, the person has to ask, "do I want to be happy?"

If the answer is in anyway half-hearted, then the desire to be free of unhappiness isn't strong and its lessons won't be learned.

If, however, the answer is a resounding "YES!" then learn the lessons of unhappiness; accord it the highest priority. Take responsibility. Investigate. Recognise the underlying causes. Be clear. Be determined. Modify the mindset. Transform your life.

If this means relinquishing expectations, relinquish them. If this means losing pride, lose it. If this means being brave, be it.

If this means apologising, then apologise. If this means forgiving others, then forgive them. If this means forgiving yourself, then forgive yourself. Forgive, not because it's necessarily deserved, but because you need to do it for yourself.

If this means living a healthy lifestyle, then live a healthy lifestyle. Eat healthily. Drink healthily. Exercise healthily. Sleep healthily.

Whatever the issue that is presented, attend to it. Do what needs to be done.

Whatever stubborn idea or aspect of ego is creating resistance, recognise it clearly and let it go. It generates unhappiness and is holding you back.

Whatever pain you harbour; let it go. There is no greater love that you can have for yourself and those around you.

⁓

The only reason you are unhappy is because of the changes you won't make.

It is a challenge and does take courage to be free of unhappiness, but there is no greater reward.

Don't cling to the lesser at the expense of better.

Don't be indifferent to your unhappiness.

43 The story of your life

Even with a strong determination it can be difficult to uncover the root causes of unhappiness.

While secondary beliefs may be revealed, it is common for underlying core beliefs to remain hidden. As such, while the experience of unhappiness may diminish it still will not be completely eliminated.

Often these deep-rooted thinking patterns resulted from early childhood experiences. They may have stemmed from a one-off incident, but just as likely resulted from conditioning over a period of time.

They may be so entrenched and may seem so natural that the person isn't aware of them ... and yet they are the source of unhappiness in their life.

While it may be challenging to uncover core beliefs, it is certainly not impossible. The key is diligence. Whatever unhappiness is experienced, learn from it. Don't ignore a single sensation. Examine the unhappiness. Trace it to its roots. Identify the underlying thought patterns.

Usually the unhappiness which results from core beliefs pervades a person's outlook on life and shapes their reaction to situations. The resulting unhappiness may be pronounced but often it is subtle, like a shadow, and may be so familiar that it isn't recognised.

While the unhappiness may be described as a pervading sense of sadness, loneliness or insecurity, an overwhelming need to be loved, or an inexplicable fearfulness of or anger with the world, it could just as readily be evidenced as general impatience or frustration, discontent or boredom, or a tendency to sulk or complain.

When this type of unhappiness is traced, the underlying deep beliefs that are uncovered are often expressed as ... 'I'm not worthy', 'I'm not good enough', 'I'm a failure', 'I should be better', 'I wasn't loved', "I'm not lovable". Alternatively, it could be expressed as a view on the state of their world, "It's not good enough", "It's not as it should be", "It's not fair", "It's not what I want", "I've been denied what I care most about".

Whatever the belief, it casts a shadow across the person's life ... even if they aren't consciously aware of the belief or its shadow.

～

However, when a person uncovers a core belief, they recognise it instantly. There is no doubt that they have uncovered a significant issue in their psychological makeup and a crucial contributor to their unhappiness.

They may be overwhelmed by the insight. It might be quite an emotional experience and they may cry.

Undoubtedly, they will feel that a major piece in the jigsaw puzzle of their life has fallen into place. They may feel very relieved at this discovery and very much at peace.

Whatever the reaction, it will be a significant revelation.

~

There is no one technique to bring these core beliefs into the light of conscious awareness, but with sincere desire the right circumstances will present themselves and the belief will be revealed. Life will present the necessary challenges that will reveal the lessons that need to be learned.

I would, however, like to share with you one exercise that you may find useful on this journey of self-discovery. The exercise is to write your emotional life history.

To do this exercise you will need to set aside a period of time – preferably when you are by yourself and won't be disturbed – to write your life story. It may take a few days or longer to complete and you may want to come back to your story several times. It's entirely up to you.

~

The idea is to write about all the significant events in your life.

You will need to describe all your experiences, noting how you felt about them at the time, what impact they had on your life, and how you now feel about what happened.

It can be useful to break the writing up into particular time frames: first write about your experiences from the ages of 0-4, then 5-9, 10-14, 15-19 and so on.

I think that it is useful if you can incorporate all the significant people in your life into your story. Describe your relationship with them, noting both negative and positive aspects of the relationship. Describe the experiences you shared with them, the lessons you learnt, and the happiness and sadness you remember. Not only describe how you felt at the time, but also how you feel now given the passage of time.

—

It can be a surprisingly challenging exercise.

The long forgotten memories which are brought up can be quite astounding, and the depth of emotion that lies buried can be a revelation. Many people aren't aware of the pain they carry with them.

However, what is most important is that each recalled experience of unhappiness should be examined carefully and traced back to the underlying belief structures. In so doing, you will gain great insights and advance your spiritual development.

Of course, if you still feel any unhappiness it indicates that there are further beliefs to be uncovered. Learn from that unhappiness; peel back the layers till you uncover the source of the unhappiness. Let nothing deter you.

~

While it may be tempting to run through the exercise in your mind, to do the exercise properly it must be written down. It is the act of writing which is extremely cathartic.

Needless to say, total honesty is a prerequisite. However, as this is a personal story there is no need to share it with anyone … unless you want to.

As the exercise is an emotionally challenging experience you may not be ready to attempt it. That's not a problem. There's no need to force anything: just note your reluctance. Understand the reasons for that reluctance.

~

I'm not saying that the exercise is essential, but it is very worthwhile. It can be very effective in bringing subconscious experiences to the light of conscious awareness and revealing deeply buried obstacles to self-realisation.

If you try the exercise and it doesn't get to the root of your core beliefs, no problem! What you will find is that with sincere desire the answers you seek will follow.

A particular situation will present itself which, if you are diligent, will give you an insight into the inner workings of your psyche. And with strong desire you will uncover those underlying beliefs.

Why not try the exercise. It is not only therapeutic, but that 'eureka' moment may be closer than you think.

44 Realise your whole self

All unhappiness is a product of the mind. If you continue to experience difficult situations in life, it points to the existence of obstacles buried deep in your psyche.

As these obstacles often arise in early childhood, it is understandable that even if you have been diligent on your journey of self-discovery, you may not be able to clearly recognise those obstacles. However, by remaining attentive to the unhappiness that is experienced, those subconscious obstacles will be revealed and resolved.

~

It is important to remember that whatever unhappiness you experience – even the most deep rooted insecurity, the most paralysing anxiety or the most profound depression – is not a reflection of you, but rather the obstacles which formed during the course of your life.

Those obstacles are not intrinsic to what you are. They are products of cultural, social, familial and genetic environmental factors.

If you didn't receive the necessary nurture and guidance for healthy physical, emotional and spiritual growth, it is likely that deep obstacles will have formed. However, while these obstacles are in no way your fault, they are your obstacles to overcome.

Getting to the root of these obstacles might seem a daunting task, but with the right motive it will happen naturally and effortlessly. Learn the lessons as and when they arise ... acknowledge, accept, explore, understand.

If you just can't identify the belief structures which give rise to the unhappiness – which may the case with 'ancestral' unhappiness (a particularly deep seated unhappiness inherited from forebears) – then focus on the sensation of the unhappiness. Feel it in your body. Observe it at length. Don't try to avoid it.

With sufficient attention either the underlying belief structures will become apparent or the unhappiness will dissolve.

⁓

Allow me to share another exercise, which might provide an interesting insight on your journey of self-realisation.

When you have some quiet time and you are sitting comfortably, close your eyes and allow yourself to relax.

When you are ready ... picture yourself as a young child. While you can choose any age, ideally start with an image of yourself when you were young ... you can then repeat the exercise with images of yourself when you are older.

Visualise this child sitting alone. Something unpleasant has happened and the child feels unhappy. The child's head is bowed, their hands are covering their face and they are clearly upset. The child is quietly crying.

As you picture this child, you instinctively understand how they feel ... maybe lonely or frightened, maybe rejected or unloved, maybe worthless or insecure. You understand intuitively.

You can feel exactly how they feel.

～

As you observe this little child, your love and empathy grows. It builds in your heart and floods through your body. Compassion wells up in you and you love this young child. You empathise with them deeply and without reservation.

You know that this child needs to be comforted and you instinctively know how to comfort them.

You walk towards the child beaming all the love and good will in the world, and quietly sit next to them.

With a little sidewards glance the child notices your presence and is so pleased that you are there. They can sense your goodwill and love. They really appreciate that you are there to be with them when they are alone and scared.

You put your arm around them and tell them not to worry because you are with them. You give them a warm hug. You feel them snuggle into your embrace and relax a little. You tell them softly that you love them. You hear them breathe a sigh of relief. You stay comforting them. They love to be with you and are glad you are there.

After being with the child for a while you ask them what the problem is. They tell you their story. You listen to everything they have to say.

You know exactly how they feel even without the words.

You nod your head and reassure them that everything will be alright.

You give them another comforting hug and tell them that you will always be with them no matter what happens. You tell them that you will always love them.

You give them all the emotional support they need and which only you can give.

You stay with this child. You know what they need – comfort, support, reassurance – and you give it to them freely, lovingly, wholly.

The child feels your love and acceptance, and loves you deeply in return. This child loves you so much ... and you love them.

Spend as much time with this little child as you like.

~

When you are ready, open your eyes.

Sense how calm and peaceful you feel, just like a weight has lifted from your shoulders.

Let yourself breathe out. Feel the love. Feel the release. Feel the happiness.

~

This little exercise can be very powerful.

Its power comes from the acceptance you give the child. However, you are not just giving the child acceptance. By loving this child you effectively give yourself the love and acceptance that you may not have received from others or given to yourself.

That love has miraculous powers to heal.

If what has been lacking in your life is due to lack of love from self or others, you may find that some of the obstacles that this created may start to resolve themselves automatically.

All you ever need is the power of your own love.

I'll repeat that. All you ever need is the power of your own love.

~

The exercise is interesting because you are both the adult who gives the love and the child who needs it. In you are both adult and child.

The child represents that part of you which perceives itself to be deficient and insecure. The adult is that part of you who can comfort the child and knows exactly how they feel and what they need.

You the child are lost; you the adult are wise. You the child are lacking; you the adult are whole. You the child need comfort; you the adult are the comforter.

~

In your daily life, it is you the child who suffers, is insecure, thinks "I'm not good enough", fears loss and rejection, craves love and acceptance, and always needs 'more'. It is you the child who refuses to forget or forgive the pain of the past.

While you remain as that child you are bound to be unhappy.

Only by realising yourself as the adult who is whole and complete, full of love, wisdom and understanding, and already possessed of all that the child could ever need, can there be freedom from unhappiness.

As the adult you are the love that the child needs.

⌣

Your whole problem is self-identification with the child.

All you need to do is realise yourself as the adult.

⌣

Love yourself wisely.

Whatever you think you lack ... you already have.

Realise your whole self and you realise you lack nothing.

45 Preparing the mind

The importance of questioning assumptions has been a major theme of this book. It is through a process of identifying mistaken assumptions that the mind is purified and self-realisation becomes possible. In this regard, we have considered mistaken assumptions relating to the nature of world and what you are, and also the cause of unhappiness.

We will continue our journey of self-discovery but our focus will shift away from identifying mistaken assumptions to the experience of a mind free of assumption … and the associated experience of genuine happiness.

This approach will take us on a journey away from the mental images which typically flood our minds, to the sensations which form the backbone of those mental images, to the underlying consciousness on which both mental images and sensations depend. Having reached that vantage we will then explore the deep recesses of the non-conscious mind, ultimately arriving at the unfathomable profundity of Reality.

The book will guide, but the journey depends on you.

With determination you will cross from concepts to realise your Reality free from all conceptual restrictions.

Unhappiness will be a thing of the past. Joy will be your moment to moment reality. Free from limiting mindsets and reactions, you will realise your passion and love everything about the life you lead.

There is nothing more that you can wish for.

~

At the outset, let me to make the point that while learned knowledge can put a man on the moon, it can't cross the chasm of ignorance which separates man from self.

If a person relies on learned knowledge, their mind will be full of the mental noise of conceptual thinking which will prevent deeper self-enquiry. Self-ignorance is an inevitable consequence.

If, however, a person relinquishes their attachment to learned knowledge and investigates the deeper recesses of mind, they will realise a profound silence. This silence will purify the mind and prepare it for a deeper and more direct search.

Free from the busyness of thinking, the mind will be infused with the wisdom of intuitive understanding. Silence is a necessary precondition for self-realisation.

~

To realise this silence it is necessary to bring the mind to a state of formless attention.

This is a natural state, but if the mind has been subject to a history of mishandling it will be restless with thoughts and feelings, and run off in every direction. Even if the person attempts to quieten their mind, they won't be particularly successful. Whatever silence they realise will be fleeting and momentary. It will be difficult for the mind to realise the necessary calmness and clarity, to experience silence.

One of the reasons why the required silence may be so elusive could relate to the manner in which it is sort. If one part of the mind tries to quieten another part, silence cannot be realised. The effort involved in subjugating one part of the mind with another creates a turbulence which overpowers any calm that is experienced.

Even in the unlikely case that silence is achieved using this method, it would be forced and not the silence that is sort.

Rather, in order to realise silence it is necessary to lead the whole mind into a state of calmness.

Many meditation techniques have been developed to quieten the busy mind – you can look at a flame, you can concentrate on the end of your nose, you can recite mantras – however, the most common is to bring the attention to the natural breath of the body. By simply bringing attention to the *sensation* of inhaling and exhaling, silence can be realised.

The technique is simple but it does require practice.

~

While you can perform this meditation technique anywhere and at any time, it is best to go to a quiet place where you won't be disturbed for 10 or so minutes.

When you are ready, get into a comfortable position. Sitting is probably best, though not essential. Try not to move during the course of the meditation.

As you may still be thinking about what has happened during the day or what you need to do later, it's good to remind yourself upfront that this is your opportunity to invest in some quiet time and that you can think your thoughts afterwards.

Give yourself this time so that you can become acquainted with that part of you which is thought-free.

~

When you are ready close your eyes and bring your attention to your breathing.

Just become aware of the normal breath in and out through your nose. Not big breaths; just normal and relaxed breathing.

Feel the breath on your nostrils. Don't think it but feel it. Notice the temperature changes in your nostrils as you breathe. Notice that it is cooler when you inhale and warmer when you exhale.

Also become aware of the sound of your breathing. Notice the difference in the hush of the breath in as opposed to the breath out.

Give all your attention to the sensation of the breath. Don't think it, just feel it.

~

Once you can feel your breath on your nostrils then follow the passage of your breath. Trace it from the nostrils to the back of your mouth, noticing the temperature changes. Concentrate on the sensation of the breath.

Once you can feel the breath at the back of your mouth, trace it to your throat. Notice the temperature changes as you breathe in and breathe out. Cooler when you breathe in, warmer when you breathe out.

Then see if you can trace the breath all the way into your lungs. Breathe in and feel the sensation of breath on the nostrils, mouth, throat and lungs. Notice the breath out from the lungs, through the throat, mouth and nostrils. Observe the temperature changes of each breath in and out.

If you can, become aware of which lung you are breathing into. Is it more the left or the right lung?

Keep focusing on your every breath.

⏝

You may find that this seemingly straight forward exercise is surprisingly difficult.

Even with the best intention, as you concentrate on your breath you may find that your mind wanders. Without even realising it, you are thinking about something else and not focusing on your breath.

If this happens, don't nourish the thoughts with interest or make any effort against them. Simply notice that your mind has wandered, remind yourself that you can think these thoughts later and return your attention to your breathing ... and the sensation of the breath in and out.

Undoubtedly your mind will wander many times. Just keep going back to the breath. The more you return to the breath, the more your ability to concentrate will improve and the deeper your meditation will become.

⏝

As your ability to focus improves, let the sensation of breathing engulf you. Be totally aware of your breath.

As your mind is taken up with the sensation of breathing, you will find that thoughts fade away. Then you become aware of a beautiful spaciousness. Your mind is serene. You are free of thoughts. It's an extremely pleasant experience ... you could even call it exquisite.

If you haven't experienced this silence before, it is quite a revelation.

⁓

Practice this exercise. Realise what it is like to be free of thoughts. Reacquaint your mind with the blissfulness of silence.

Just by meditating each day you will not only feel calmer and more relaxed, but more remarkably, this simple little exercise has the power to change your life in ways that you couldn't have dreamed possible.

As the silence purifies your mind, life will become simpler, clearer and less stressful. And as your mind is given space from conditioned ways of thinking, deep insights will dawn on you and previously unanswered questions will be resolved.

You will also find that with concerted meditative practice that what is really important in your life comes into clear focus and you effortlessly direct your attention to those priorities. Naturally, you find the time and space to enjoy and pursue your true passions.

As you persist in meditation, you will reach the stage where mental silence is your daily reality. Having embraced this silence, your life is filled with peace, love, happiness and freedom. You are in harmony with everything.

~

Practice is the key.

Just from practicing this simple exercise you can free your mind from the mental noise to which you may be accustomed. The resulting benefits can be incredible. The miraculous starts to happen.

The investment of your time is small: the payoff is great. Incorporate this simple exercise into your daily life, it will be one of the best things you do.

~

When the mind is clear, everything is clear. That clarity comes with silence.

In that silence you grow in wisdom: it is the spaciousness in which discovery happens.

To realise your reality, first realise this silence. It is the prerequisite for self-realisation.

46 Deepening conscious awareness

While the breathing meditation is highly beneficial, it isn't a goal in itself. It is just one of many techniques aimed at rehabilitating the mind.

If you have been able to realise that inner silence during meditation, don't stop there. Be persistent and build on that achievement. Become aware of that silence in your daily life.

The more you can become aware of the silence beneath the mental noise, the more you can improve the purity of mind. And the greater the purity of mind, the more conducive the conditions for self-realisation.

～

Focus on the sensation of breathing as you go about your daily activities.

Be aware of your breath when you are walking, standing, reading, waiting, doing household chores, or even when you are talking to other people. You can even do fairly complex tasks and still maintain awareness of the breath.

What can be difficult is to remember to focus on the breath. Time and time again you will forget. However, each time you do, make a note that your mind has wandered and turn your attention to the breath again.

The more you practice this exercise, the more your mind will be introduced to the beauty of inner silence and the more it will be purified.

Make it a habit to become aware of your breathing and to realise the silence which is always there.

⁓

This exercise is beneficial because it not only promotes serenity in your life but also broadens your field of conscious awareness.

As you practice the exercise, you will become aware of two levels of conscious awareness. On the one hand, you will be aware of the usual mental images which pop in and out of your mind (the thoughts, feelings and experiences) but on the other hand, you will become aware of the less obvious sensation of breathing. While that sensation is always there, it is, by and large, overlooked ... usually because of those other more active mental images which hijack your attention.

By becoming aware of this less obvious sensation you deepen your conscious awareness. It is no coincidence that the more attention you give the sensations which underpin the usual run of mental images, the more you move into silence and purify your mind.

Awareness of sensations you take you one step closer to the realisation of your reality.

~

By extending the exercise, you can deepen your conscious awareness even further.

Once you are consciously aware of the sensation of breathing then also become consciously aware of other sensations.

So if, for example, you are walking, become consciously aware that you are walking. But more significantly, become aware of the sensation of walking. Notice the sensations which occur in your ankles, knees, hips, spine, shoulders, elbows and wrists as you take each step. Become aware of the muscles you use in your legs, arms, torso and neck. Become aware of your whole body. Observe the sensation of walking in its entirety. Don't think it, feel it.

Then, while you are deeply focused on the sensations of walking, also become aware of the sensation of breathing. Be aware of the sensation of each breath as it is inhaled and exhaled. Be deeply aware of both the sensation of breathing and the sensation of walking at the same time.

The more you practice the easier it will become.

~

A further step in the exercise is to not only be consciously aware of the sensation of breathing and whatever you happen to be doing ... but also aware of the sensations of your environment.

When you find yourself in a given situation be aware of what is happening around you. Be aware of the sensations of what you see and hear, what you smell and what you are touching. Be aware of the sensations on your skin – the sun, the breeze, the temperature, the clothing you are wearing. Become aware of every sensation. Think about those sensations, but more important than that, feel them.

As much as possible become aware of the totality of your sensations. Focus on your sensations without losing your awareness of any others ... from your environment, your activities, your body or your breath.

See if you can uncover the peaceful silence that underpins all that you experience.

—

Having mastered awareness of your sensations, you can then extend the exercise further. When faced with any situation make a full note of what you experience.

Become fully aware of the facts of the situation. Notice how you feel and what you are thinking. Be aware of your impulse to react.

Don't own what you observe; just make a mental note of it. Be objective and not particularly interested.

Be acutely aware of the entirety of your sensations … the sensations that come from your environment, the sensations of your actions and the sensations of your breathing.

Realise the silence beneath everything you experience.

⁓

When faced with challenging or demanding situations this exercise can be very daunting, but they present excellent opportunities to practice and learn.

Be aware of the situation and, in particular, what you are contributing to it. Be fully aware of all your sensations.

Observe. Do not try and control. Just observe.

If you are in a highly charged emotional state this can be an extremely difficult exercise, but with practice you can realise the silence beneath even the most challenging situations.

⁓

With practice you will not only reach the stage where you are consciously observing your sensations but you will be aware that you are observing them. You won't just observe your thoughts, feelings and reactions but you will be aware that you are observing them.

By observing, you go beyond the thinking and feeling mind and deepen your conscious awareness.

The hallmark of that awareness is the profound peacefulness of the thought-free state: silence.

~

Practice is the key.

Use every experience as a means of deepening your conscious awareness. Observe all that crosses your field of attention but don't own any of it. Realise the distance between you and whatever is experienced. Be aware of all but don't own anything. Look at all from the outside.

Appreciate that whatever you observe, you are not that, but that which is observing.

~

Dispassionate observation prepares and purifies all aspects of mind.

The more you observe, the more peaceful your mind and world become, and the more realisation becomes attainable.

Be aware of the mental picture which forms in your mind but be especially aware of the sensations which underpin the mental picture.

Step back and observe ... whatever follows will be beneficial.

⁓

Be conscientious in your practice of these exercises, but remember that being consciously aware is far more important.

47 Now is the doorway to self

Having deepened your sphere of conscious awareness and realised a level of calm silence, the mind should be ready for a deeper search.

In the past couple of chapters our focus has been on weening the mind off its attachment to mental images by encouraging awareness of the underlying sensations (which themselves are a more rudimentary form of mental image) and from that vantage, introducing the mind to the thought-free state of silence.

In this chapter we will continue the exploration of the mind by introducing awareness of 'now'.

Just as what you are can't be found among any of the mental images which populate your mind, your reality can't be discovered in either the past or the future.

It can only be realised in the split moment of 'now'.

'Now' is crucial to self-realisation. Now is the doorway to the self. Now is the journey of self-discovery.

⌐

But what is 'now'?

If a person understands 'now' as the mere passage of time from the past to the future, they will have difficulty appreciating the significance of 'now' and why it is of any use to self-realisation.

There are 4 points that I would like to make in relation to the phenomenon of 'now'.

⁓

The first is that 'now' is much more than a mere passage of time … it is the only time. It is always now. It was now 5 minutes or 500 years ago and will be now in 5 minutes or 500 years' time.

Everything that has ever happened and will ever happen, happens at the moment 'now'. That is, whatever happened in the past happened when it was 'now' and whatever happens in the future also happens when it is 'now'.

Even memories of past experiences and plans about future experiences happen 'now'. Everything happens 'now'. 'Now' is not a mere passage to delineate past and future, it is the only time that there can be. It is the only moment.

⁓

The second point is that 'now' isn't a momentary appearance squeezed in between past and future. Instead, it is an unbroken moment.

It is the continuous moment which supports all appearances of past and future. It is the all-pervasive moment from which past and future emerge.

It underpins all time, and yet it is so fine and subtle that it can't be discovered in time. 'Now' isn't in time ... past and future are in it. Without 'now', there is no past or future.

'Now' is the source of past and future.

~

The third point that I would like to make is that 'now' has a different quality about it to both past and future.

Even though the past was 'now' and the future will be 'now', 'now' is neither the past nor the future. It isn't even affected by the appearance of past or future. 'Now' is perennial, it doesn't change.

'Now' has the stamp of the actual, the sense of being real. 'Now' is alive and vibrant. 'Now' is timeless and fresh. 'Now' is new. 'Now' is endlessly creative. 'Now' is life. 'Now' is love and happiness. 'Now' is the taste of eternity.

~

The fourth point is that while 'now' is ever-present it can't be grasped by the thinking mind.

While past and future may seem to be independently existing phenomena, they are actually mental images. They are mental experiences which appear and only exist 'now'.

However, unlike the past and the future, 'now' can't be conceptualised. As soon as you try, it immediately becomes the past, which is not the 'now' you are trying to grasp. Try again and the same thing happens. No matter how hard you try you can't conceptualise 'now'. 'Now' is elusive.

While the thinking mind can easily picture the past and, by projecting those memories, imagine the future, it isn't the right instrument to comprehend 'now'. It can only understand 'now' as a passage from the past to the future. It can't fathom how all time can only exist 'now'.

~

Awareness of 'now' is the next step on the journey of self-discovery.

Past and future are of no use for self-realisation. What you are can't be found in time.

You only need 'now'.

~

While 'now' can't be grasped with the thinking mind, it is perennially available. Regardless of where you go or what you do it is always 'now'. 'Now' is your constant companion.

Once you become aware of the ever-present moment as your direct experience, your spiritual growth will flourish.

Discover it for yourself. Stop being distracted by concepts of past and future; let your mind be quiet and still. In that silence, 'now' is self-evident.

In the clarity of 'now' the self is revealed.

Now is the doorway to the self.

48 Beyond time is being

The mind which shuttles between its ideas of past and future is spread in time. If you give your attention to the noise of mind you will not realise 'now'. Your body, on the other hand, is spread in space. It only exists 'now'.

As such, by bringing your attention to your body you are drawn out of time and into 'now'.

If, for example, you think about rubbing your hands together, your mind is projecting a possible future. If you think about having rubbed your hands together, your mind is conjuring the past. However, if you rub your hands together and feel a sensation of warmth and energy, that sensation is the sensation of 'now' … but as soon as you think about that sensation; the 'now' is lost.

'Now' must be approached as a sensation and not a thought.

Why? Because it is a sensation and not a thought.

In this chapter, and with the benefit of having practiced some basic meditation techniques, you should be ready to explore the 'now'.

﹏

As you read and concentrate on these words you are probably not aware of your feet. They are always there but unless they are causing you some discomfort you are unlikely to be aware of them.

In this exercise I would like you to bring your attention to your feet. I don't want you to think about them: I want you to sense them. You can start by feeling your feet as they touch the ground, but I want you to uncover a more subtle sensation. Try and notice the sensation of having feet ... of having skin, muscles and bone. Identify the sensation which tells you that your feet are alive.

The sensation that you are trying to uncover is similar to the sensation you feel when you rub your hands together, however, it is much more subtle, at least initially. I would describe it as a warmth, an energy, a vibration, but you can use your own words.

To become aware of this sensation, your mind needs to be quiet. If it is calm you will be able to focus and you will be able to uncover it quite readily. If you have difficulty, practice the breathing meditation first and then bring your attention to your feet. If you are having particular difficulty, it may also help if you bring your attention to one foot at a time.

~

This subtle sensation is the sensation of 'now'. It is always there, but while you are caught up in ideas of what you have done and what you must do you will overlook it.

So, the next aspect of the exercise is to maintain awareness of your feet as much as possible during the course of the day. Be aware of the sensation of having feet when you are walking and sitting, talking and eating. You will forget them many times, but every time you realise that you've forgotten, notice that you've been caught up in thoughts and bring your attention back to your feet.

At every opportunity, become familiar with the sensation of having feet.

Having practiced the breathing meditation it should be a fairly simple exercise. After some practice you should start to feel the vibration in your feet quite strongly.

—

The next step is to trace that sensation throughout your body. Feel it in your ankles, calves and shins, knees and up to your hips. Feel it in the left leg and right leg, and then both legs together.

Notice the sensation in your stomach and chest, and feel it running through your lower, middle and upper back. Feel it in your abdomen and all along your spine. Become aware of the sensation in your shoulders and trace it down both arms to your hands.

Also trace the energy into your neck. Feel it in your scalp, forehead, cheeks, nose, mouth and chin.

Sense the energy throughout your whole body.

~

It may take several sessions to experience this energy throughout your body ... it all depends on how clear and relaxed your mind is to start with.

The sensation is always there though. You just need a quiet and attentive mind to uncover it. If you are in a sufficiently peaceful state, the life force in your body will be very apparent.

Having stabilised in that state, you may then find that you experience a very strong and almost overpowering energy. Not dissimilar to an electric current, it may dance throughout the whole of your body or energise particular parts. You may find that this 'special' energy heals body and purifies mind, sparks profound insights, enhances intuition and helps you realise subtler levels of being.

First though, uncover the sensation of your body and experience it at every opportunity. Make it a habit to sense it at the start and end of each day, and as much as possible during the day.

Stay with this sense of 'now', it will introduce you to all the experiences necessary for your journey of self-discovery and will ultimately lead you to the self. 'Now' is both way and guide.

—

As you become familiar with the energy of the body, it will become apparent that this sensation of 'now' is nothing but the sense of existence ... the feeling of being alive. To be is to be 'now'.

This sense of being is, in fact, the sensation of consciousness at the root of your conscious mind. It makes all your other senses possible. Everything in your world is dependent on it.

If you don't have this sensation then you don't know you exist and nothing else in your world is possible.

—

Furthermore, the sense of existence can't be discovered in any of the mind's ideas. It is only realisable through the body at the point here-now. When you experience the sense of existence it is here ...and it is now.

Conversely, when it is here-now you experience the sense of existence. The reason for this interdependence is that the sense of existence is the sense here-now.

As such, the reason why it is always here-now for you is because here-now is your sense of existence. While you exist, wherever you go it is 'here' and whenever you go it is 'now'. You define here-now by existing ... by just being.

We might add that inasmuch as the sense of existence is consciousness ... consciousness is here-now. As here, it is spaceless. As now, it is timeless.

⌒

Shift your attention from thoughts to sensations ... from past and future to now ... from mental images to the core mental image ... from ideas to existence.

Don't think ... just be. Don't be this or that ... just be. Be without the ego.

Stabilise in the sense of existence. Surrender to it. Let it completely engulf you.

In that silence, the fact that you are will open to what you are.

Understand existence ... and all is resolved.

49 A guided meditation

Picture yourself taking a stroll in a park one beautiful spring morning.

You come to an inviting sunny spot and decide to catch up on some reading. As you sit down you feel the warmth of the sun and hear the relaxing hum of buzzing insects.

You are cajoled into closing your eyes and enjoying the moment. Every now and then a cloud momentarily passes in front of the sun and you notice the buzz of insects subside.

You become aware of the faintest of breezes rustling the blades of grass and gently cooling your skin. When the cloud passes, the sun emerges and once more your world heats up and the insects resume their busyness.

You note the shifting sensations of your body and the meandering thoughts of your mind ... and recognise them as an intrinsic part of this beautiful spring morning.

～

You become aware of this mental picture in its entirety and observe it from a distance. It becomes increasingly dreamlike.

You allow your attention to move to your body and your sense of being. The more attention you give it, the stronger you can feel it grow.

You let the life force in your body engulf your attention. It is a very enjoyable and satisfying experience.

～

You slowly open your eyes and gradually observe your world around you ... ensuring that you remain mindful of your sense of existence.

You become aware of the sensations in your body. You feel your legs and arms, abdomen and neck. You feel the ground beneath you. You observe the sounds you can hear. You note the shapes and colours you can see.

As your world comes into focus, you remain attentive to your sense of being.

As you observe, you notice that everything is in a constant state of change ... your world, your mind and your body. Then it dawns on you that among all this changefulness that your consciousness is the one aspect that hasn't changed. It is the constant factor in a world of changing appearances.

～

It becomes apparent that your sense of being is the foundation of all your other sensations. You know that without it there are no sensations or mental images. All is dependent on existence.

As you remain aware of your sense of being, you recognise it as the continuity which bridges all the changing mental appearances that make up your world. It is the glue which binds all else in your world together.

You know that your consciousness makes all else possible. You know that without it nothing is ... and that your mental image of you is not. You recognise that all hangs on the thread of your conscious awareness.

~

As you become increasingly aware of the subtle but powerful energy of being, it solidifies to become the undisputable reality of your life.

It is the constant factor. All else is merely changing appearance playing out on the dimensionless screen of your mind. It is the anchor in a sea of fleeting sensations.

It is the foundation of the mental image which is your world. That foundation is your being: all else is its expression.

~

As you stabilise in your being, everything other than consciousness is seen as external to you.

Even your innermost thoughts and feelings which fuel your mind, the sensations which define your body, and the breath which gives them life are recognised as external to you.

They are an intrinsic part of the mental picture of your world ... but not what you are.

You identify with being and know all else as a mere state of mind.

⌣

The more you are conscious of being, the more you realise that it hasn't changed throughout your life. It was the same when you were a child as now that you are an adult.

Your body, self-image and experiences have changed, but being remains the same. It is unaffected by thought or feeling, pain or pleasure, age or infirmity.

Even in dream all may be different but your sense of being remains the same. It is the one constant in life.

All changes in the light but not the light itself.

⌣

The more conscious you become of your sense of being the more you recognise it as the one incontrovertible fact in your life. It is highly significant.

Whether sitting, walking, eating or reading, stay with your sense of being. Recognise it. Explore it. Be it.

Distinguish existence from experience.

Without awareness of being you cannot expect to have any realisation of what you are ... and must remain lost in that constantly changing picture which is your body, mind and world.

—

To recognise being as the only reality and all else as temporal and transient is freedom, peace and joy.

Abide in your sense of existence.

50 Consciousness as subject

Your sense of existence is the only constant in your life, but while your attention is consumed by the changing mental images which fill your mind, it will be overlooked.

Even if you are vaguely aware of your sense of being, you will not appreciate its significance. Instead, any understanding you have about yourself will be dominated by those mental images of the person you think you are and you will not be able to understand how you could be anything but a real person living in a real world.

While you lose sight of your sense of existence you will have trouble conceiving that everything that you think you are is just a mental appearance ... and not what you are.

However, once you stabilise in the sense of existence it will become clear that the person you have taken yourself to be is a mental formulation which only exists in your mind. And you will realise that more than the changing appearance of the person, you are the 'changeless' consciousness.

It becomes apparent that as the consciousness you are the subject, while the changing appearance of the person is a mental object you observe. Because you observe that mental object you know that you can't be that person.

~

If you haven't done the meditation exercises and explored your sense of existence this will be a difficult concept to grasp. Actually, it can't be understood by just reading words. You must explore your reality for yourself. There is no substitute for direct experience.

Without that experience you will not be able to differentiate consciousness from the mental image ... and because of your attachment to the mental image, will not be able to comprehend that the person you think you are is just an object you observe.

~

While direct experience is the best teacher, the following example may help explain the point.

One day Mary, who believes that she is a person, is walking down the street and meets Bob, who also believes that he is a person.

Mary has the sense of being the subject of the encounter and perceives Bob as the object (not in a derogatory sense, just meaning that he isn't the subject). Bob has a similar experience. He assumes that he is the subject and that Mary is the object.

While Mary has the sense of being the subject, she appears to Bob as an object. Similarly while Bob has the sense of being the subject, he appears to Mary as an object.

This example is indicative of the fact that every person has the sense of being the subject, but appears as an object to everyone else.

This raises an interesting question ... how is it possible? How is it that everyone has the sense of being the subject, while at the same time appearing as the object?

What is the actual situation? Is Mary the subject and Bob the object? Or is Bob the subject and Mary the object? Or are they both subjects? Or perhaps both objects?

If one is subject and the other is object ... which one is which? And how do you know which one is which?

～

I guess that you could try and explain the situation by arguing that perspective determines whether something is the subject or object. That may seem a persuasive approach but it does raise the question ... how is it possible that a mere change in perspective could change anyone's reality from subject to object?

Either Mary is the subject (in which case no amount of changing perspective will alter that fact) or she is just imagining herself to be the subject (in which case a shift in perspective will reveal her true identity as an object).

The same applies to Bob. Either he is indisputably the subject or he is just imagining himself to be the subject.

⌐

A different explanation is suggested when the puzzle is considered from the perspective of consciousness. From this perspective, the solution is clear: both person Bob and person Mary are objects.

Any confusion only arises because Mary and Bob assume that they are the subject. In actual fact, the subject is neither the person Bob nor the person Mary ... but the underlying consciousness.

Bob is an object to Mary, Mary is an object to Bob ... and both Mary and Bob are objects of consciousness. They are mental appearances which appear to the consciousness.

⌐

If Mary comes to realise herself as consciousness and not the mental image of the person ... then she will not only observe person Bob as an object, but she will also realise that the person Mary is also just another object.

Similarly, if Bob realises himself as consciousness, person Mary and person Bob will also appear as mental images and, therefore, objects under observation.

From the perspective of consciousness, persons Bob and Mary are only objects imagining that they are subjects. In actuality, the subject is neither of those mental images, but the root consciousness.

~

The person exists as a succession of mental images. As a purely mental phenomenon it only exists as an observable object to the consciousness.

While you think you are the person, you will confuse what is actually an object as the subject.

That misunderstanding is entirely due to a failure to investigate the nature of your consciousness and its relationship to the mental images of you the person.

~

To understand, you must explore for yourself.

Don't rely on these words. They are not sufficient.

You must understand for yourself ... not conceptually, but as your direct experience.

51 Consciousness is one not many

Your sense of consciousness is clearly crucial to everything in your life.

It is only because you are conscious that you can have sensory experiences, perceive mental images and realise that you exist. That consciousness is not just one sensation in a mind full of sensations; it is the primary sensation. It is the sensation on which all others depend. It is the subject sensation; all others are objects.

This relationship can only be fully appreciated through persistent meditation. It must be your experience.

⁓

If your consciousness is the subject of what appears in your mental world (including the mental images you have of yourself and others) it still leaves the question, what is the relationship between your consciousness and the consciousness of the other person?

Is one consciousness the subject and the other the object? Are they both subject or both object?

What is the connection between your consciousness and theirs?

⁓

To answer this question, let's start by considering your own consciousness.

As you read these words, the reason you know you exist is because of your sense of existence. That sense is the only proof you have that you exist. Without it, you would have no idea whether you exist or not.

However, your consciousness is such a profound proof of the fact of your existence that at no time can you meaningfully say that you don't exist. Even if you were convinced that you don't exist, the fact that you were convinced would only serve to confirm that you do! How else would you have the belief?

While you might not know what exists, without doubt you do know that you exist.

So the first point that I'd like to make is that the fact of being conscious is proof of existence.

~

While that sense of existence is definitive proof that you exist, it is only valid for you. The sense of existence you experience does not prove to other people that you exist.

Although anything that you might say or do to convince others of the fact of your existence might be very compelling, it only amounts to a collection of ideas to them. Crucially, as mental images those ideas are not proof of existence.

The only proof of existence is the sense of existence ... which is something that you can't convey. As such, you cannot definitively prove your existence to anyone else.

Similarly, no one else can prove to you that they do exist. Whatever they say or do will only appear to you as a mental image, which does not amount to proof of existence ... and certainly not proof of existence separate to yours.

Actually, rather than prove their existence, the mental images you form will only serve as further evidence of your existence. The only reason that you can have those mental images is because it is you who exists.

So the second point is that there is no proof of existence other than the sense of existence. Ideas don't prove existence.

~

While you can infer the existence of others, you can't prove it. Others can infer your existence, but can't prove it. The only existence that you can conclusively prove is your own. The only existence that anyone else can irrefutably prove is their own.

As existence must be experienced to be proved, you cannot conclusively verify another existence other than your own. Any idea about the existence of a consciousness separate to your own is only an inference and not a proof.

~

This raises an interesting, but crucial, question.

Why is it that you can't prove another existence or consciousness separate to your own?

Intensive meditation reveals an answer which might seem counter-intuitive.

The reason why an existence or consciousness separate to your own can't be proved is because it doesn't exist. Your consciousness is all and total.

While it may appear that many individual life forms possess their own individual consciousness, it isn't like that. Consciousness is, in fact, one. The existence that you sense is the same existence that is sensed by everyone else. It is the one consciousness expressed in multiple forms.

The belief that your consciousness is individual to you is mistaken. That consciousness is in fact common to all.

Consciousness, existence, being, presence (however you like to describe it) is one and the same. The sentience in all sentient beings is one. The 'I' in the sense 'I am' is the same.

⁓

The implication is that in any interaction between two people, while different images may appear, the underlying consciousness is the same ... the life in the life forms is the same.

That underlying reality is the subject of all mental images which appear in any number of worlds. There may be an infinite number of objects but there is just one subject ... and it doesn't change with perspective.

Everything is an object in appearance, but is the one subject in essence.

—

The more you meditate, the more evident the situation becomes.

Experience your consciousness. Investigate it and you will realise that your sense of existence is all there is. There is no other.

As you stabilise in consciousness, ideas of you and me are negated. In consciousness there is no sense of me and you ... there is just existence. That existence is one and all. The existence in you is the existence in me and the existence in all life forms.

Life is one ... not many.

—

Even the appearance of seemingly different people is recognised as the one mental phenomenon.

Despite the appearance of separate bodies and separate minds, there is no boundary separating bodies or minds;

there is no start or finish of any body or mind. And what has no boundaries has no separation.

What appears as various mental images is actually one and the same, observed by one and the same consciousness.

As the issues raised in this chapter stretch the intellectual mind's ability to understand, I strongly urge you not to rely on my words. Explore for yourself. Be conscientious in your meditation. Broaden your conscious awareness. Understand your existence directly. It is the only way.

52 Existence is only a sense

You say "I" many times during the day ... but what exactly do you mean by that word?

Certainly, you have the sense of existence and, therefore, know you exist ... but what is it that exists?

You appear as body, but that appearance is in the mind. So are you a mental image?

No doubt, the mental image cannot exist without consciousness. So, are you, in fact, consciousness?

And even though consciousness lights your world, you experience it as a sensation ... the sense of existence. Are you, therefore, a sensation?

And if you are a sensation, even a significant one like existence, what are you when you aren't conscious and don't sense anything?

What is your reality?

⁓

Several chapters back we noted that you cannot be the body or a mental image, but we didn't consider whether you could be the consciousness. If, for the moment, we assume that you are the sense of existence, what would that mean?

Well we could say that while you exist here and now, you are not anything that appears in space or time. As the essence of body and mind, you would be neither body nor mind. As consciousness you are not a walled phenomenon. Being formless you are neither entity nor individual.

You give life, but are nothing that you give life to. You create, but you are none of your creations. You can be experienced but you are beyond the thinking mind.

~

That would be the case if you were consciousness. However, can you be so sure that you are the consciousness? Would it be a mistake to assume that you are the sense of being?

Let's explore this consciousness in a bit more detail.

While your world is predicated on the experience of consciousness, it is, however, only a temporary phenomenon. During the course of a 24 hour period the sense of existence appears and disappears. It appears when you are awake and continues while you dream, but in that dreamless state of deep sleep it disappears.

For a significant part of each day the sense of existence goes into abeyance. All is put aside and forgotten.

There are no mental images of self or world. You are not even aware that you exist. By simply lying down and closing your eyes in sleep, your sense of existence goes into oblivion. Sometimes you experience consciousness, sometimes you don't.

The fact that consciousness comes and goes indicates that there is a deeper reality underpinning its appearance and disappearance.

In addition, while the sense of existence does not change throughout life, when you examine the sensation closely it becomes apparent that it is not constant. Instead it has the consistency of a vibration; rather than being continuous, it flickers. There are gaps in the stream of consciousness.

This raises the question as to what exists in the gaps between each infinitesimal flicker of consciousness. Indeed, on what is consciousness predicated?

Having observed that consciousness is both temporary and intermittent, we can observe that it must be an expression of a deeper pre-conscious reality.

As such, we could say that it arises from a confluence of conditions occurring at a pre-conscious level. It is a product of non-conscious functioning which, nevertheless, is sufficiently aware to ultimately manifest as conscious awareness.

When the appropriate conditions arise, consciousness is experienced, bringing with it the sense that you exist. When those conditions dissipate, the consciousness subsides, taking the sense of existence with it.

~

It is true that when consciousness is experienced it may seem very real; however, it is actually nothing more than a sense ... the sense of existence.

Undoubtedly it is a significant sense – the foundation of the senses – but, ultimately, it is just a sense.

It is a product of conditions ... a mere appearance to be understood and appreciated while it makes its appearance. Although it is a highly valuable tool, it is not the ultimate reality.

~

The conclusion that must be drawn is that, despite the paramount importance of consciousness in your life, you are not the consciousness. You experience the consciousness, but it is only a sense which appears to you.

You experience that sense, but you aren't that sense. It may be the only proof that you have of your existence, but it isn't your underlying reality. There is a deeper part of you which exists when you don't experience consciousness.

In fact, there are great pre-conscious depths to your reality.

⌣

We know that this is true because when you are in a state of deep sleep and have no conscious awareness, there is a deeper part of you which sustains your body and allows you to waken when called.

In that state you are aware, but not consciously aware. You exist, but without the sense of existence. Actually, there is no question of existing or not existing; there is total freedom from all sensations and ideas. It is an embryonic consciousness ... a seed-form of being. It is the first taste of self beyond being.

You may not be able to recognise it while asleep, but when you waken you can readily infer its existence. That aspect of you doesn't go to sleep. It is always awake. It is always aware.

Even though you may not have considered this aspect of self, nevertheless, you know it exists ... it is your deepest mystery.

⌣

That non-conscious state is the support for consciousness, body and mind. In that state the conditions of consciousness are reenergised, and body and mind are refreshed and rejuvenated.

That prior state is so significant that if consciousness does not go into abeyance and revert to that prior quiet state, the life form will not survive. It will become ill and die in a matter of weeks.

⁓

Consciousness is only a condition – a mere quality – that appears to you. You are not that changing condition, but that to which the consciousness appears.

To understand, you must explore for yourself. Words alone only create ideas and are not the understanding you need.

In search of self, realise what is known. Recognise that you are not that. Go deeper and realise unknown layers of being. Recognise that you are not that.

Continue with your search. Once you can go no further, you will realise your reality beyond being.

53 Existence as object

When you meditate on the sense of being you realise that it is everything. Yet despite its vastness you still cannot discover what you are. You quickly realise that while the sense of existence will tell you where to look, it is not what you are looking for.

At first your attention is taken with the staggering beauty of being, but as you stabilise in that sense you become more familiar with its nature. You then realise that despite its vastness you are actually observing it. Incredibly, there is a distance between you and the sense of being.

As you become more and more aware of that distance, you awaken to the fact that you aren't the sense of being, but that which is observing it.

It is a terrific revelation.

~

While words cannot do justice to this revelation, it may be useful to picture the sense of being like a cloud in the sky.

When you first become aware of the cloud it envelops you to such an extent that it appears that you are that cloud. However, the more you observe the cloud, the more you realise that there is a distance between what you are and what you observe. It then dawns on you that you aren't the cloud but the spacious sky in which that cloud appears.

It is through the existence of the cloud that you become aware of the existence of the sky. Ironically, without the cloud you would not have awareness of the sky.

~

Once you perceive yourself as the sky then it becomes clear that the sense of being is just an appearance in the immensity of sky.

Whereas consciousness was once perceived as subject and everything else as mental objects, it too becomes another mental object under observation.

It may be the root mental object, the foundation of all mental objects ... but it is still a mental object.

~

It requires an intensely peaceful state to witness existence, but once being is observed, you are beyond it.

Through profound observation the sense 'I am' dissolves to reveal the observer of 'I am'. That observer is transcendent.

~

That state of pure observing is indescribably beautiful. It is powerfully pure, peaceful, quiet and calm. Existence is frenzied in comparison.

It is rich with the subtlest love and happiness. It isn't blankness but an exquisite understanding. It is pure understanding without knowledge ... knowing without anything being known.

It is a vast emptiness but so full and rich with potential.

It is unimaginably whole and complete.

It is the ocean of mind.

There is limited value in describing it. The true value is in experiencing it.

⁓

Once experienced you realise yourself as the observer of all. You know that you have always been the observer and all else has merely been observed.

As the ultimate subject of all that happens, you are not one among many, but the uniting factor of every appearance of diversity.

All exists in your observing, is one in your observing and only exists as your observing. Nothing greater than you the subject observing it.

Absolutely everything you observe – whether concept or consciousness – you are not that ... yet, indisputably, you are.

～

As observer you are the changeless background against which all changes are perceived.

Just as space remains unaffected by everything that appears in that space ... so you remain unaffected by whatever is observed.

All changes without changing you. You are neither shaped nor affected. You don't develop or decay. You are completely unattached.

You are the constant factor at the root of all appearances.

～

As observer there is no limitation or imperfection. You are indisputably whole and complete, and all is recognised as whole and complete.

Limitation only occurs when part is seen in isolation from the whole. Then imperfection is inevitable. However, when the whole is perceived then nothing is seen in isolation ... and there is no limitation.

As observer, there is whole perception and no misunderstanding.

～

I have used the word 'observer' for ease of communication, but if it creates the impression that there is an actual observer which observes, it is misleading.

In actuality there is no entity or presence which is observing ... there is just observing. There isn't something which perceives, there is just perceiving. There isn't something which understands, there is just understanding.

To imagine that observing is the act of an observer would be a false assumption. There is no observer observing anything.

Much more than an observer you are the observing.

⁓

Once there is whole perception, any notion of observer and observed merge in the observing. All is just observing.

The appearance of what is observed is seen as the expression of the observer, and the appearance of the observer is seen as the expression of the observed. Both are expressions of observing.

While the appearance of observer and observed may change, observing doesn't. Despite the appearance of change there is the clear realisation that there is no change.

Everything changes without anything changing. And what you are changelessly you are that beyond doubt.

—

Observing is the first glimpse of self beyond being.

54 Beyond being ... the pathless path

Realising the unchanging oneness of everything is the highest state of spiritual practice. It can be realised through intensive meditation. It may take months or years, but it is possible.

While it is a blessing to reach this deeply blissful state, even so, your reality is still not revealed. The state represents an opening in consciousness, the first taste of the real ... but it is not the ultimate.

There is a gulf between this state and self-realisation ... the realisation of Reality.

~

This gulf cannot be crossed by meditation, prayers or worship.

No technique or activity, practice or discipline can reveal it. Self-realisation is not a reward for good behaviour or long endured penance. It can't be obtained or earned through effort or diligence.

Your Reality can't be realised through worldly or spiritual knowledge. It can't be grasped conceptually, nor is it reachable by any sensory experience.

Changes don't bring you to your natural changeless state. You are already beyond all change.

~

There is no path to this ultimate state.

You can't reach it as a goal, because you already are it. If you try to reach it, you won't realise it ... the trying makes you miss it.

All you can do is work on the obstacles to self-realisation and ensure that your mind is clear. While there is no causal connection between your attempts and realisation, the obstacles can be deeply affected.

Once those obstacles are dissolved you realise your Reality. Your obstacles are the only problem. There are no bridges to cross, just don't maintain the chasm.

~

Self-realisation can't be compelled or willed either. Forced effort at the level of the mind is unnatural and will only serve to obscure it.

It must sound like an impossible task, and while it is seen as a task it is impossible. However, when the conditions are right, realisation will occur naturally.

Just as flowers blossom or fruit ripen without effort, and as all rivers in the absence of obstacles return to the ocean, so your reality will dawn and you will realise yourself beyond being.

~

Perhaps the key ingredient is desire.

You must desire to know your truth and that desire must burn within you. A passing interest isn't sufficient.

With desire that last obstacle which divides inner from outer and separates conceptual from non-conceptual will be dissolved.

Without desire, the ultimate won't be realised.

~

That desire must be pure.

If the desire is tainted by motivation for recognition or the belief that special powers may come from enlightenment, then it isn't pure and will serve as an obstacle to self-realisation.

Enlightenment must be wanted only for its own sake and not for any other purpose. There can be no harbouring of any desires for material or spiritual benefits resulting from enlightenment.

The desire must flow from a well of selfless love. That is the true motive. From that love, self is desired for its own sake. Happiness is only incidental. Reward is not contemplated.

~

Purity of desire brings an undivided heart; free from inner contradictions and incompatible desires.

With the requisite purity of desire you live an integrated life. Your behaviours don't belie your beliefs and your goals are in harmony with your way.

You are sincere in your thoughts and words, and your actions are free of stereotyped gestures. Nothing you do is done for show or recognition.

You are absolutely honest with yourself and your desire is reflected in selfless diligence and dedication.

Every aspect of your life is your practice ... every experience is as an opportunity to learn.

~

If you are blessed with mindful alertness and a sincere desire for truth, all will happen automatically.

You will have the perceptiveness to recognise all assumptions which obscure your reality and the courage to clear your mind of them.

Your progress will be inevitable.

You will apperceive the infinite and what lies beyond. Your reality will be clear and your search will be complete.

‿

There is no transition to your ultimate Reality ... you simply realise you are it.

55 The seeker must dissolve in the seeking

If you are an earnest seeker, perhaps the greatest obstacle to self-realisation is the idea that you are a seeker ... an individual entity in search of Truth.

To realise what you are, abandon all attempts at self-definition. Be free of all distinctions and boundaries. Recognise no limitation.

~

While there is an entity seeking enlightenment ... its search will be fruitless.

No matter what that supposed entity has, thinks or does, it can't perfect itself into an enlightened being. Regardless of what is achieved that 'entity' can't comprehend its source any more than a shadow can understand its substance or an object can know its subject. It is a mental image which can't comprehend itself in the absence of that mental image ... yet that is what is necessary for enlightenment.

~

For enlightenment, it must be realised that the idea of a separate entity is a mistaken assumption; its appearance an illusion.

There must be absolutely no doubt that there is no entity which can be enlightened. The slightest idea that there is an entity of any description is an insurmountable obstacle to enlightenment. Assuming what you aren't blinds you to what you are.

Enlightenment isn't of the entity, but from the idea of being an entity.

⌐

While there is an individual meditating, trying to understand, and working towards self-realisation, there can be no enlightenment.

You are not a person or individual entity, and can't be enlightened as one. The idea that you are a person, body, mind, spirit or entity of any description is a misunderstanding.

The mental image of self is not your identity. It is not your Reality.

Don't adopt the pose of an individual ... there can be no real understanding as an individual. You aren't an individual and can't be conceived as one. Stop believing what you are not.

Apperceive at the deepest level that there is no separate self. Refuse to consider yourself as anything.

⌐

While the seeker is happy in its pose as a seeker it can't realise what it is seeking. The seeker must disappear. And in the absence of that obstacle what you are will become apparent.

While blinded by the personal, the universal can't be perceived. Only once the pseudo-identity dissolves can there be the realisation that there is no 'you' to realise anything.

Without the idea of the false entity you are simply what you are. There is no entity which is enlightened. There is no entity in need of enlightenment. There is no entity.

‿

While the term "self-realisation" has been used as a means of communication throughout the book, the irony is that there is no self.

There is neither a self to realise anything, nor a self to be realised.

That said, there is realisation, but it is the realisation that there is no self. Realisation is not of the self, but from the idea of being a self.

‿

While 'you' think you have understood … you haven't. There can be no understanding while you think that 'you' have understood. That 'you' must go.

Anyone can reach that state which is … but no one can reach that state which isn't.

56 Complete surrender

The realisation that there is no individual entity is the unequivocal acceptance that there is no 'you'.

Having relinquished the idea of being an individual, there is no 'you' who can claim ownership or responsibility for anything. There is no 'you' to do anything. There is no 'you' to act or cause others to act. There is no 'you' to influence events. There isn't even a 'you' to play a part in life.

Whatever action occurs doesn't happen by, to, or even through the illusory 'you' but is the result of an inevitable chain of causal events stretching the length and breadth of the universe, of which, ultimately, 'you' have no control.

Without that 'you', whatever you once thought you did is seen as an expression of the functioning whole: a universal succession of events.

～

While you think you are an entity, thoughts seem to be personal to you; but when the person disappears then the thoughts are recognised as products of universal processes.

They appear to you, but are not your own. They arise from forces beyond your control: neither personal nor deliberate, they merely happen.

Even now, if you trace the origin of those thoughts to their source it should be clear that they originate from the broader environment (non-conscious and conscious) and not from you, the individual.

⏤

Once the non-existent entity is eliminated it becomes obvious that your so-called will is just the inevitable. Whatever you may think or do is the unavoidable.

You realise that you aren't master of what happens: all is part of the total functioning. What must happen has happened and will continue to happen.

Whatever 'you' think or do is an expression of that total environment. Whatever changes 'you' try to make are part of that same expression. Nothing thwarts the inexorable expression of the total functioning.

⏤

While the world may be full of action, no actors are involved. If anything is achieved it is not by individuals, but by the total functioning.

Trying to understand in terms of individuals or entities thinking or doing anything, is an obstacle to realisation.

You aren't an individual doing anything. There are no individuals or entities to do anything.

Whatever you observe appears to you but it is entirely the expression of universal processes ... appearing to universal processes.

—

Don't own your thoughts and actions. Observe them closely and see that they are reactions. Trace them to the environment. Realise that they are external to what you are.

Broaden your field of awareness; become aware of the functioning of the whole; realise all as just universal processes playing out in the ocean of mind.

Know that whatever happens is an inevitable expression of what must happen.

—

Observe but don't take ownership. Don't think "I am doing this" ... rather, observe and realise that all is just happening.

Don't say to yourself "I am observing" but rather "there is observing". Accept a passive role and distance yourself from the actions of the individual. Be neither cause nor recipient.

Similarly, when meditating don't think "I am meditating", rather just note "there is meditating". The purpose of meditation is for the "I" to go. Eradicate the individual from the equation. "I" is an unnecessary inference and causes nothing but confusion.

Be free of action. Leave all to the total functioning of which body and mind are an intrinsic part.

Let the actor dissolve into the action. Observe the action but don't hold onto the acting.

—

Enlightenment can't be an act of volition.

The least effort will prevent what otherwise happens naturally and spontaneously. Trying is the obstacle.

All effort must cease. The focus is on freedom from doing. There is nothing to be done and no one to do it.

—

Deliberately not doing something will also prevent realisation. There must be both total absence of doer and total freedom from doing.

Complete surrender is necessary.

Just be.

57 The price of the infinite is the finite

Spiritual maturity lies in the willingness to let go of all obstacles.

Make your life your practice.

Welcome life as it comes. Don't ask or refuse. Accept all and resist nothing. Know that what will be, will be ... and know that you need nothing else.

Flow with life. Let all pass freely, don't hold onto anything. Use but don't possess. Live without burden. Learn from every unhappiness.

Be present in each moment. Don't make anything a means to something else. Let all be its own means and purpose.

Give up preconceived ideas. Don't have firm rules about what should or shouldn't happen. Be free of expectation and anticipation.

Face tasks calmly. Don't procrastinate nor assume control or responsibility. Be aware of what needs to happen and let it happen.

Enjoy and admire all with affectionate detachment. Don't get caught up or involved.

Observe body and mind, and see that they are moved by forces beyond your control.

Be unconcerned with cause and effect. Don't be proud of achievements or embarrassed by failures. Leave success and failure to the unknown.

Abandon self-interest and personal ambition. Act without selfish motive. Filled with enormous goodwill, expect nothing in return. Live for truth, not profit or pleasure.

Don't strain towards the future or ask what's next. Don't be impatient or in a hurry. Free of all tangible objectives, let each day be a journey into the unknown.

Just be aware. Whatever you hold onto serves to limit you. It is your obstacle to overcome.

Only when all is given up can you move beyond, then you know that there was nothing to give up.

Relinquish even the most sublime ideas about what you are. Even the deepest flashes of insight must go. Just be.

Discard even the idea that you haven't found the self and all will come into the focus of direct perception. You already are what you are. You know it, you just haven't realised it.

Make your life your practice.

58 Enlightenment

When the known is completely investigated it dissolves, bringing you to unknown layers of being.

Go further and the unknown will explode, shattering all.

～

Those last steps are made in silence and solitude. You are revealed in total silence.

When you experience that inner emptiness, the explosion of Reality is near.

～

The preparation may be gradual but enlightenment is sudden and complete. It is a momentous and unmistakable event. There is no doubt as to what has happened. It can't be compared with anything.

You are immediately silenced and astounded.

～

All is liquidated. Inner and outer dissolve. There is no separation or division.

The absolute absence of everything is realised.

~

The peacefulness is all encompassing.

The silence is deafening. The stillness is profound.

~

There is incredible lightness and clarity.

Understanding becomes so subtle it disappears. Everything becomes clear and obvious.

Direct understanding is a revelation. It is exquisitely beautiful.

~

In the absence of all ... your Reality is clear and obvious. It is instantly recognisable. It isn't what you expected but it is what you have always known.

The direct experience of self is natural ... but astounding.

It is something completely new but, paradoxically, so familiar. You have intuitively always known what you are ... you just overlooked it. You realise that you never lost yourself. You are as you always have been. You have always known, but now you realise.

You are amazed that something so obvious has remained obscured for so long.

~

Once self is realised there is no need for definition or conceptual understanding. You are the non-conceptual Reality. It is so obvious, but so unexplainable with words or ideas. Concepts can't do it justice. They can't even approach it.

You are absolutely nothing ... an unimaginable emptiness. You are formless, dimensionless, spaceless, timeless, everythingless ... but unbelievably rich, full, complete and total.

You are unfathomable silence, absolute stillness, profoundness beyond imagination. You are infinite and unlimited but impenetrable and incomprehensible.

You are all that has ever been desired.

~

Any description is misleading. You are forever beyond the furthest reaches of the mind.

~

You can only know self by being self. There is no other way.

'Self-realisation' can be the only understanding of what you are.

~

Once you realise your reality, there is complete acceptance that you are neither tangible nor intangible, yet you are all there is or could be.

~

You are the reality which lies beyond all. You don't come from that void and nothingness ... you are it.

You are that supreme Reality ... that limitless being beyond being.

59 Nothingness is all

Once self is realised, nothing is the same again.

From the perspective of self, all is seen in a fresh light. A range of insights and revelations are experienced which are startling in their depth and profundity.

Your world takes on a dream-like quality and your life changes in ways that you never could have believed possible.

The changes are a direct result of your heightened understanding or, more precisely, your decreased misunderstanding.

The perspective which comes from self-realisation never leaves you. The resulting life changes are irreversible. Your life is never the same again.

Over the next few chapters, I will share some of the perspectives which may result from self-realisation and the changes to your way of life that may occur.

～

When the nothingness of the self is realised it is recognised as the only Reality. There is only the nothingness and void of the self.

You are all and total. There is nothing but you.

~

You realise that you are that incomprehensible potential out of which all worlds emerge. They appear as an infinitesimal drop in the vastness of what you are.

That nothingness, which is you, is not an appearance in any universe ... all universes are appearances in it.

Everything arises out of nothingness, has its source in nothingness and is in essence nothingness. Everything is the expression of your nothingness.

Nothing is separate to your inherent Reality. Nothing can be separated from you.

~

As the reflection of nothingness, everything is the reflection of you. All derives from you.

Trace anything to its source and you, the inexhaustible potential for everything, are there.

You are the unfathomable centre of everything. Everything owes its existence to you.

You can't be found in anything ... everything can be found in you.

~

You recognise that all is your creation. You create and illuminate all.

You don't do anything but all happens naturally, effortlessly and spontaneously ... just because of what you are.

You make all possible.

⁓

All worlds are created, but not your Reality. You are before and beyond.

You are the immovable and unchanging source which underpins all.

⁓

It is clear that your Reality is expressed in your world, making your world seem real. More than that, it is expressed in an infinite number of worlds, making all those worlds appear real.

However, nothing in those worlds is real. Those worlds are dream-like images which appear, change and disappear.

They appear real, but they aren't. You don't appear, yet you are real.

⁓

You realise that whatever appears, you are not that.

Just as the sun is everywhere in light but isn't that light, so all is your reflection but you aren't that reflection.

You are in everything you observe but you aren't what you observe.

All is an expression of what you are, but as an expression is also a limitation of what you are.

~

When investigated, it is apparent that the entire universe results from observing being expressed as observer and observed. Observing, observer and observed are indivisibly one.

As the inconceivable potential which makes them all possible, you are altogether beyond.

They are perceivable objects ... but not you. You are imperceptible: imminent yet transcendent.

~

As Absolute, you are neither subject nor object ... but you manifest as subject and object: subject in sensation, object in appearance.

As subject, you are reflected in all objects. As object you are reflected in all subjects.

Absolute subject and absolute object are the same. You are that Absolute non-subject, non-object.

~

You are the source of now, expressed as space and time. Your body is space. Your mind is time.

All bodies in space and all minds in time are yours. They appear as many, but all are one. That oneness is a reflection of you.

You, on the other hand, are neither body nor mind. You are not space nor in space. You are not time nor in time. You are absolutely timeless and spaceless.

You are beyond dimension and all comprehension.

~

As nothing is you, you are nothing. Yet your nothingness is the richness of everything.

At the level of mind there can be no understanding, but from the perspective of self all becomes apparent.

60   The dissolution of concepts

Your natural 'state' of nothingness is absolutely devoid of concepts. There is no duality of mind and matter, nor knowledge and no-knowledge. There is no who or what to understand, nor anything to be understood.

Primitive but complex concepts stir, then consciousness bursts on you and you know you exist. You have no control over its appearance. Being neither willed nor wanted, it isn't a volitional act. It happens without your consent.

From the moment of this birth you become conscious of sensing, perceiving and experiencing. Memory is created and soon a world built out of knowledge emerges, complete with a you who lives in that world: a person with a body which grows and acts, and a mind which thinks and feels.

~

The entirety of this world exists as an appearance in consciousness. It appears in the conceptual volume of space and conceptual duration of time, but only happens here and now. Seeming real, it exists as a mental image.

The consciousness assumes the identity of the person and spends its conceptual life trying to achieve what will make it feel happy. It seeks the usual symbols of happiness – gets a job, buys a house, gets married and has a family.

In an attempt to understand the world it lives in, the person may be drawn to ideas from science, religion and spirituality to explain its existence and bring a sense of meaning.

Regardless of the explanations – which can be detailed, intricate and even compelling – they are just ideas made possible by the appearance of consciousness.

~

At some point during the fleeting appearance of consciousness, the dreamed entity feels unhappy. It attempts to escape the shadow of its suffering, but no matter where it turns in its dreamed world it can't realise lasting relief.

With a flash of insight, the dreamed entity turns its attentions from the dream to the dreamer and enquires into its own reality. It explores through its own experience rather than through a veil of learned ideas until one day it breaks the conceptual shell in which it had been entombed and reality comes rushing in.

World and entity is realised as dream. Its reality is not, however, that dream, but the nothingness beyond all dreaming.

~

The world becomes increasingly dreamlike ... all swirls like a cloud, lacking depth meaning and purpose.

All hangs on a strand of consciousness. The illusion of an independent world of solid objects is shattered.

Patterns of order and chaos are recognised as patterns of mind. All only exists as it is perceived.

All is contained in multiple mental universes existing simultaneously: unique, but without separation or independence.

⏤

The illusory actor acting in an illusory world is perceived and identification with that false mental image dissolves.

There is indescribable freedom. There is no 'you' to do anything. All is observed nothing is owned.

⏤

The entirety of conceptual appearance is perceived.

The beautiful pattern of events – appearing, merging and disappearing – is observed from the perspective of self. And that distance brings a profound understanding.

You know that nothing is. All is illusion and nothing really happens.

⏤

The non-conceptual Reality is realised and apperceived as 'self' ... and there is no need for conceptual understanding.

You realise there never was a need.

61 The cycle of life

From the perspective of the conscious mind, nothingness is the unlimited potential for everything. It is everything in a latent state ... and infinitely more.

In the stillness of that nothingness, awareness stirs and a speck of 'something' appears. It is a conceptual appearance and is the natural expression of that nothingness.

That something takes shape as the duality of 'I' and 'not I'. It represents the birth of mind and matter. Mind is subject 'I': matter is object 'not I'.

While mind and matter appear to be separate, in actuality they are indivisible. They are two aspects of the one. Together they comprise the entire universe.

⁓

Through the non-conscious interaction of matter and mind, evolution occurs ... subatomic particles appear as planets and atoms appear as life forms.

All appears to be spread in time; however, all only happens now. All appears to be spread in space; however, all only happens here.

Following the appearance of the root mental image 'I am', a pattern appears which is interpreted as a person living in a world. As a result of focusing on the part at the expense of the whole, the mistaken idea 'I am that person' forms and suffering is born.

The evolution from nothingness to the person is not a conscious process. It occurs naturally. There is no control over the process. The process is the control. All happens as it happens.

Any attempt at controlling the process is just the process at work.

~

The appearance of anything in this process is a product of the prevailing conditions. It is dependent on the conditions and only lasts while those conditions prevail.

Nothing exists independently of its conditions or autonomously to them. Every appearance is an inextricable aspect of the environment from which it appears to emerge.

When there are atoms there can be elements: when there are elements there can be living organisms: when there are living organisms there can be consciousness.

Only when there is consciousness can there be a world of mental images, which includes conscious sensations and concepts about atoms, elements, living organisms and consciousness.

While the organism is alive and conscious, the respective mental world appears. However, when it is alive but not conscious (as in a state of unconsciousness or deep sleep) the conscious world disappears. And in the absence of consciousness, there is no world of sensations and concepts. It can't exist.

If the necessary precondition isn't met the product can't result.

~

The appearance of a person is just one of many mental objects which appear in a mental world.

The person appears as a result of consciousness and disappears without it. When there is no conscious awareness, the person doesn't go anywhere, it just ceases to appear.

Once those conditions re-emerge and consciousness is reactivated then the mental person and its mental world returns.

~

In the case when the organism is no longer alive and breath departs the body, a similar process occurs.

In the absence of a living body, consciousness is no longer supported. Without that consciousness there is no sense of existence, no sense of being, no idea 'I am'; there are no sensations, no experiences and no world.

The person with its thoughts and feelings ceases to exist.

—

At the moment of so called 'death' the person doesn't go anywhere. In the absence of the right conditions the mental picture of the person simply dissolves.

As the stream of consciousness drops away, being recedes into non-being and becomes unfelt. What appeared to be, no longer appears to be. The sense 'I am' gives way to 'I' … and only the non-conscious functioning of mind and matter remain.

Like a drop of water merging with the ocean, the illusion of the person finally dissipates.

Appearance meets reality, infinity is embraced and the person disappears forever.

—

Then the mental image of the person only survives as a mental image in the minds of other people … where its sphere of influence multiplies or dwindles.

The body of the dead person appears as lifeless and is disposed of. However, life still continues in the body ... the ageless functioning of atoms and elements continue unconcerned by the departure of consciousness and breath.

The body decomposes as a natural function of the process and in time the material of the body is transformed into new life forms.

Life prevails.

—

Non-conscious functioning results in both the appearance of consciousness and its disappearance. The conditions change but the functioning continues.

Even if the greatest calamity occurs, the functioning continues quite uninterested ... bridges are built out of obstacles. In point of fact, there is no calamity.

When one set of conditions ceases, another set continues. What appears to be exhausted actually becomes expansive.

—

Everything that is born must die.

Death, however, isn't the end ... it is just one aspect of an ongoing process. For anything to be born there must be death. Death is necessary for renewal. The price of birth is death.

Birth and death are the cycle of life. Life remains.

—

Ultimately, whatever appears must disappear. Whatever is done must be undone.

The birth of the universe is the promise of its death. Whatever comes must go.

In the end all appearances will be dissolved … leaving neither gain nor loss. All accounts are squared.

Nothingness is the ultimate Reality ... just as it always has been.

⁓

There is no choice … no guiding hand.

What comes uninvited departs uninvited.

All happens as it must.

⁓

And what of you?

You remain as you always have been. What you are was never born and can never die. What you are neither appears nor disappears.

You aren't anything that appears at birth, changes throughout life and ceases to be at death.

You are the origin and end of all. You prevail above and beyond.

All else goes but you prevail eternally. You are the changeless source of all changes.

—

Everything appears, lasts its duration and dissolves … but you aren't bothered.

You aren't affected by the appearance of anything. You are beyond whatever happens. The conceptual never touches you.

Despite the departure of the body or the extinction of the universe … you are as you always are … immutably you.

—

To believe yourself to be born is the promise of death.

To know yourself beyond being is immortality.

62 Liberation

Self-realisation is irreversible.

Once ignorance is transcended and your reality explodes into the light of conscious awareness, you never forget what you are.

Through constant awareness of what you are, you stabilise in the Ultimate. You never confuse or mistake your Reality.

You have the unshakeable conviction that you are the Absolute.

You are never lost again.

~

This enlightenment brings with it a completely fresh perspective which ushers in spontaneous yet profound changes to your attitude and motivation, character and approach to life. You appear the same but nothing is as it was. You are liberated.

These changes are genuine. They occur naturally; no effort is involved. They are deep and lasting.

~

Following 'self-realisation', remaining traces of the problematic mind are identified and unhappiness is dissolved.

You experience a sense of fullness and completeness that is so natural that it permeates your life totally. It is so much a part of your daily experience that you aren't aware of it ... till you think about it.

There is a very clear sense of not wanting or needing anything, because you already have everything.

You are deeply, completely and profoundly happy, calm and peaceful. You are what you are and that is all and sufficient.

There is no shadow of individual existence. Suffering and unhappiness exist as a vague memory.

You are total. You are whole. You are complete. You are all. You are one.

⁓

The body and mind continue their functioning, but are perceived in their correct perspective.

Thoughts, feelings and actions are recognised as links in the chain of universal causation. As aspects of the total functioning, they are observed but not owned. The whole is not subsumed by the part.

There is the realisation that body and mind are ruled by circumstances beyond their control. Doing as they must, they attend to the practicalities of life.

You are not caught up in the activity of body and mind. Instead you calmly observe the resolution of all.

You observe all fall into place as it should and must. You witness the beautiful dovetailing of events.

Life becomes simple and easy.

⌣

From the perspective of self, there is joyful non-attachment.

Without particular attachment to the body and its associated experiences, there is true bliss. Having no sense of achievement or frustration, you welcome all experiences and are in harmony with whatever happens.

You are vibrant with life but deeply serene. As the world neither holds nor binds you, you are free.

You have no worries or problems. There is no self-concern. You can't worry even if you try.

⌣

You know that everything will turn out as it must.

You are content with whatever happens. All is accepted and appreciated for what it is.

Expectations are dissolved. Fears and desires disappear. Nothing is wanted, nothing is rejected.

You are free from having to control anything and have little interest in meddling in the course of events. You are happy to watch all unfurl.

～

There is no specific intention in daily life. You live in the moment. All happens as it must.

You are at one. You are at peace.

You watch all fall neatly, smoothly and rightly into place. Just by being, all is taken care of.

You are so much in control that you don't need to control.

～

Your mind is cool and clear, quiet and alert. All is perceived intuitively and directly.

Everything is clear. There is nothing to bother you.

Clarity of mind is normality.

～

You are total in every moment. You think, feel and act in harmony with the whole.

Your actions grow in understanding and clarity, purity and selflessness.

What is done is done for others. There is no room for selfishness nor is there a clash of interest between self and others.

You live an integrated life.

By realising what you are, everything is changed.

~

As you experience the love of being, that love radiates like a light shining on all.

It isn't selective or intentional. It is love as action not reaction.

It isn't tainted by self-interest, desire or selfish motives.

The love for all is pure because it is the love of self. It is love beyond form and words.

~

You are ruled from within not from without. You go where life takes you.

You have the courage to believe that you are free and act on it.

Life is a journey into the unknown ... and it's great!

⌣

Happiness, peace and love are so natural that only by comparison with the past can you recognise the change.

Living with realisation is liberation.

Nothing more could you want for yourself ... or those around you.

63 Making world right

Heaven and hell are expressions of mind.

You can attempt to make your world a better place by earning money, doing charitable activities, trying to gain influence or power. However, if your mind is not right, nothing will be right.

If your mind is not clear your world will reflect that lack of clarity and no matter where you go or what you do the problems of mind will follow you.

A mind riddled with misunderstanding must inevitably produce a world riddled with problems and unhappiness.

～

Whatever problem you observe in your world is symptomatic of problems in your mind.

Rather than try and improve your world, attend to the real cause of the problem – your mind. By transforming your mind you transform your world.

Only once your mind is right can your world be right. When the mind is clear all is clear.

～

If your mind focuses on the part it will see a world of chaos and suffering. However, when the whole is perceived, there are no problems.

By perceiving the whole, you don't change the part but your perspective ... and this change of perspective changes everything.

While you picture yourself as a separate entity existing in a real world, a limited perspective is inevitable. However, by realising what you are your perspective is complete. Then there is no chaos or suffering and all resolves effortlessly.

From the vantage of 'self' all happens as it should and must – rightly and properly – just as it always has.

∼

Significantly, you can be of no greater help to your world than by putting an end to your own misunderstanding.

While your mind remains as it is, then so must your world.

∼

Only once you have made your own mind right are you in a position to be of genuine help to others.

Then you recognise that the real cause of anyone's problem lies with the mind.

Misunderstanding is the problem; recognition of that misunderstanding is the solution.

The best help that you can give is to point out the source of their problems. The rest is up to them. Either they will listen and take action or they won't.

That's not saying that you should be indifferent or unsympathetic to another's suffering. To the contrary, if your heart tells you to help then help wholeheartedly.

~

However, if anyone is to realise a world of peace and harmony they must first realise it in themselves.

Inner harmony is the prerequisite for outer harmony.

Transformation must start with the mind.

If the mind isn't right, heaven will be perceived as hell.

~

Self-knowledge is the cure for all problems.

To be a light is to know what you are.

Realise your reality!

64 Realise Self

You can have many ideas of good and bad but they are just mind determined values ... mere products of convention and culture.

There is nothing objective about these values – they are situation dependent. What is perceived as good by one is perceived as bad by another.

Change the scale of values and the idea of good and bad changes with it.

Inasmuch as good and bad are ideas, they have no existence beyond the mind. However, putting that caveat to one side, I want to suggest a measure of good and bad which is applicable to every situation that can be encountered.

Good is what promotes realisation. Bad is what prevents it.

Good is the recognition of mistaken assumptions. Bad is the stubborn attachment to mistaken assumptions.

＝

The fundamental good that you can wish for yourself is the blessing which follows from self-knowledge.

There is no greater love than the desire to know what you are. There is no greater love for self or world than to realise what you are.

⁓

What are you?

A sense? An idea? An image?

Do you exist? Or is that a sense you have? What are you without the sense of existence?

What are you in the absence of your ideas and concepts?

These are serious questions that deserve careful consideration. In your lifetime, you owe yourself complete resolution. Don't settle for anything less.

What exactly are you? Beyond words, beyond ideas, beyond sensation?

⁓

Throughout the course of this book I have used many words in an attempt to stimulate interest in the self ... and you can trust what I say. I speak truthfully.

However, whatever you do ... don't believe me!

Scrutinise and examine every word ... and then discard them. They are of no use to realisation.

Your truth can't be captured by ideas. You must explore for yourself. If not, all is in vain.

No one but you can answer these questions.

It is your journey.

⁓

Question your assumptions. Nothing is as it appears.

Recognise your unhappiness. Embrace it, observe it, learn from it, be free of it … all of it.

Realise that self-knowledge is what is missing in your life.

Appreciate all that you aren't.

Meditate. Realise the silence beneath the noise.

Be aware of your sense of existence. Stabilise in it.

Expand your field of conscious awareness.

Observe all. Expect nothing.

Accept what comes, especially when uninvited.

Make your life your practice. Nothing less will suffice.

Be whole and complete: know no separation. Be integrated with all.

Don't hold onto anything ... including these words.

~

The complete realisation of what you are not leads to enlightenment and liberation.

Go beyond whatever you perceive or conceive ... you aren't that. You are the unfathomable foundation of all.

The task may seem hopeless. But with a pure heart all obstacles will be overcome.

Love works tirelessly for your ultimate good and through that love the abyss which separates you from what you most seek in life – 'you' – will be crossed.

~

There is no reward for knowing what you are ... the realisation of what you are is the reward. Once self is realised all else follows.

~

I wish you the blessing of self-realisation.

You are what you seek.

~

Know yourself beyond being.

About the author

Born in Tasmania, Australia, Thane practised as a legal professional. A series of profound epiphanies radically transformed his life, prompting extensive overseas travel and intensive exploration of mind. The results were remarkable. As he describes, the shell in which he had been encased was cracked and inner and outer were dissolved ... he was all, nothing and beyond all and nothing. A family man, he now resides in Sydney, travelling to South America on a semi-regular basis.

Front cover

Developed from the concept of self-similarity, the fractal is a mathematically generated image. Describing many irregular structures in nature (otherwise indescribable by conventional mathematics) the fractal has been called the thumbprint of god.